TENNIS
FOR
WOMEN

TENNIS
FOR
WOMEN

Doubleday & Company, Inc.
Garden City, New York

Our thanks to James Hambuechen, president, and Maureen
O'Keefe of International Professional Consultants; to Peachy
Kellmeyer, Virginia Slims Tennis Circuit tour director; to
Ellen Merlo, of Philip Morris; and to Steve Flink, of *World
Tennis* magazine, for their cooperation in preparing this book.

**Published by Doubleday & Company, Inc., Garden City,
    New York 11530**
Printed in the United States of America

Contents

Foreword

Women's professional tennis is the youngest of the major sports and one of the most successful. About ten years ago, there was only $2,000 in prize money for the months of September through May for women tennis pros, while during the same period the men tennis professionals were competing for $250,000. The amount of prize money had changed dramatically by 1973, when the women were competing for almost $1 million. By 1979, the figure was nearly $3 million.

Until late 1970, women tennis players were always relegated to the backcourts at tournaments and were scheduled to play in the early morning hours. Today, they are playing on front courts in prime time, they receive star billing in the Civic Center, the Forum, the Coliseum, and the Garden, and the stands are packed when they compete. But the gals had to go on their own, in an all-women's pro tour, to show the world that women's tennis was a tremendous attraction.

The players who wrote this book have, over the years, been among the top performers on the Women's Pro Tour. Each is, or was, a star in her own right and a superb competitor. Each devoted many years to practicing four to five hours a day, seven days a week, but such dedication does not necessarily make a champion. For every tennis player who succeeds in international play, several thousand others fail at different levels of achievement. It takes more than practice to get to the top; it requires natural talent, dedication, the will to win, concentration, perfect technique, and confidence.

Wendy Turnbull was voted the Women's Tennis Association's Most Improved Player award by fellow players in 1977, a year in which she jumped from number 30 in the international computer rankings up to number 9. Two years later she had climbed to number 7 and had won the Wimbledon doubles in 1978 and the U.S. Open doubles title with Betty Stöve in 1979. Her remarkable quickness afoot has earned her the nickname "Rabbit."

Nancy Richey has had a glorious record. She has four times been ranked number one in the United States and has six times been U.S. Clay Court champion. She has wins over most major international competitors, and in five matches with Chris Evert, Nancy was undefeated. Nancy, despite her small physique, is one of the hardest hitters in the women's game, cracking ground strokes from corner to corner and constantly catching her opponents off balance. She learned the game from her father, George Richey, one of the best teaching pros in the country, and she practices regularly with brother Cliff, also a distinguished playing professional.

Val Ziegenfuss, a U.S. Wightman Cup player, has the best overhead in women's pro tennis. Val is a beautiful and graceful woman, and she epitomizes the serve-and-volley attack. She is one of the most attractive athletes in any sport, an elegant example of cinema good looks and tennis prowess.

Wendy Overton, a stunning blonde, started her professional career as a lowly qualifier on the Women's Pro Tour in the summer of 1971. By the end of 1972, she was ranked in the first ten of the world—a tremendous achievement in such a short span of time. Despite some injuries that have curtailed her play, Wendy is one of the hardest workers on the tour.

Rosie Casals of San Francisco can hit any shot in the book, plus two hitherto unknown. She is one of the smallest of the women pros on the tour and by far the most acrobatic. Despite her size, she is a fantastic leaper and volleyer, capable of hitting shots from behind her back, between her legs, and around her neck. She

and Billie Jean King have often been rated the number-one doubles team in the world, and when Billie Jean is not available, Rosie can win a title with any one of a dozen women. In singles Rosie has also stood out. In 1972, she won more prize money than any other woman pro in the world with the exception of Billie Jean.

Karen Krantzcke of Australia, until her tragic death in 1977 the tallest woman on the tour, had a pulverizing game. She clouted her forehands, bashed her volleys, and crushed her overheads. Yet she was capable of playing with the greatest amount of caution when she knew that that method would win for her. Karen had to fight illness in her battle to get to the top, but in spite of poor health, she managed a world's first ten rating and scored over almost every top competitor.

Kerry Reid, a beautiful Aussie, has the best sidespin forehand in the game. In 1972, she was rated number two on the Women's Pro Tour. At the U.S. Open at Forest Hills that year, she beat Chris Evert to reach the final. She was also a finalist in the $100,000 Virginia Slims Championships at Boca Raton, played in October 1972. In 1973, she was the finalist to Margaret Court in the first four tournaments on the women's circuit. In 1978, she won the Wimbledon and U.S. indoor doubles, and then was a doubles finalist in the U.S. Open with Wendy Turnbull.

Lesley Hunt, another Australian, is a super athlete. In her first year on the Women's Pro Tour, she knocked off almost every top player, and she has overcome her one weakness, a short second serve. In 1979, she won three doubles events with teammate Sharon Walsh.

Françoise Dürr, singles champion of France, winner of the French, Wimbledon, and U.S. Open doubles, is one of the headiest, cleverest players in the game. Her strokes are anything but classic, and she has a backhand that is all her own, but for tactical skill in singles or doubles, she is unsurpassed. She has a rather soft serve, but no matter how hard the opponent cracks it, Françoise always manages a superb volley. She has regularly ranked in the world's top ten and is also one of the top doubles players in the world.

Betty Stöve, a warm, friendly Dutch woman, won the Grand Slam of doubles in 1972, taking the French, Wimbledon, and U.S. Open titles. Betty is a standout in doubles but almost as good in singles. No one is quicker than she at net and no one volleys harder. In her hot streaks, she can also make placements from the backcourt on the slowest of surfaces.

Kerry Harris was also one of a brilliant group of Aussies on the Women's Pro Tour until she retired from competitive play in 1975. As the partner of Kerry Reid, these two Kerrys made an extremely solid combination. She had the perfect build for tennis—tall, thin, and flexible.

Everyone enjoys watching the superwomen stars of tennis because they combine so well technical achievement with tactical skill. Even under bad conditions—in winds of 40 miles an hour, under a midday blazing sun, or even under bad lights—each point is skillfully worked. It is as though one were watching chess in action rather than slam-bang, all-or-nothing power tennis. Even the biggest serves are returned, errors on return of serve are rare, and long, subtle rallies are frequent. When watching women's tennis of this level, one sees every shot demonstrated to perfection, and one then understands the tremendous amount of work, determination, and skill that goes into making female tennis stars.

GLADYS M. HELDMAN
Publisher, *World Tennis* magazine

Introduction

Women's tennis has changed dramatically since the start of the Virginia Slims circuit in late 1970. There are more women than ever before both successfully making, and trying to make, a living from professional tennis. Accordingly, women's tennis has acquired a new depth, simply because more women have been given the opportunity to play in tournaments. The up-and-coming players learn a lot by competing against, practicing with, reading about, and watching closely as the top women professionals play. The competition is extremely fierce and aggressive, and the fitness of the women is at a very high level. But each tennis player has attained her level of play not because of natural ability alone, but because she has worked hard at her game.

Tennis for Women is written by women who have made tennis their profession, especially for women who want to know how to play better tennis. As you read its chapters, you will notice the great variety in the advice they offer on strategy, style, and teaching methods. This advice is given by athletes who have played tennis most of their lives, have themselves received similar advice, have experimented and practiced, and have finally decided upon strokes that they think are suited to their abilities and their games.

But this book is intended to be read not only by women, but by men as well. Why? Women in general are not as strong as men, so their tennis is not a game of power. Rather, it is a game of strategy and finesse, a style of play that spectators can readily observe and from which all players can easily learn. Lacking comparable strength, women depend more upon tactical skills and on moving their opponents around the court as much as possible. Watching one of our matches, you will notice how each player attempts to play to her opponent's weakness, putting her on the defensive. You will also see power serves, ground strokes harder than you can imagine, and aggressive styles of play. Mostly, though, you will see that women rely upon strategy to win their points, which is a skill that all tennis players need.

As professional tennis players, the women who contributed the chapters of this book and I know what other women are capable of doing in tennis; you who read it should benefit greatly from our experience. I know, personally, how much my younger sisters', and even my older brothers', games improve after I have given them a few helpful hints—and they enjoy their games more afterward, just because of a little advice.

When you observe a tennis tournament, whether it be a men's or women's event, you observe firsthand that each player's game and strokes differ. Grips, strokes—backswing and follow-through—and even footwork are groomed to the individual. There are always several ways to hit each shot, but the important thing to remember when playing is that you find the shot that feels natural to you. Don't try to hit a shot that doesn't suit you simply because your favorite tennis player hits it well. I am convinced that there is no perfect way to hit a shot. I have seen some absolutely fantastic shots played, and they were perfect shots by the person who played them because they were right for that particular player's game. So, remember that the stroke should feel comfortable to you.

Most of all, learn to enjoy playing tennis and you have learned a lot. I am sure that none of us could play tennis as much or as often as we do if we didn't enjoy it. Tennis is a game for everyone—from the elderly to the young, athletes and non-athletes. It is a sport that grandparents can play with their grandchildren, and it is a good social game. It can also be a very competitive game. Of course, if you are competitive, it becomes a psychological game, a test of confidence and the will to win. But no matter what level of tennis you play or how competitive you are, it is important that you enjoy the game.

Tennis is also a game that can be played one-on-one or as a team, and it depends upon the players which game they prefer. Most professional players compete in both singles and doubles. Singles is an individual's game, one player's ability and mental strength against another's. Playing doubles is, on the other hand, considered more relaxing and is a totally different game from singles. Here, everything is teamwork, and to enjoy and play good doubles, you must find a partner with whom you combine well and have a good time.

Remember, the professionals who contributed to this book have played tennis nearly all their lives, and with great success. Most continue to do so. It takes a lot of hard work and dedication, many victories and defeats. Read what they have written, find the strokes and styles that suit you best, and if you want to improve, practice. But most of all, enjoy our game!

WENDY TURNBULL

The Backhand
by Wendy Overton

Start with the most basic, most
natural, and easiest stroke in tennis.

Born in 1947 on Long Island, New York, Wendy Overton grew up in Ormond Beach, Florida. She was introduced to tennis at age 11 when her mother suggested that she attend a 25-cent, Saturday-morning tennis clinic. From there she went on to be ranked fifth nationally in the 18-and-under category in singles and first in doubles with Mary Ann Eisel in the same category.

Although she continued to play tennis at Rollins College, where she earned a degree in history and public affairs, Wendy was, by her own admission, more interested in other things. After two years as managing and teaching pro at Linden Hills Indoor Tennis Club in Bethesda, Maryland, Wendy joined the professional circuit.

Once on the circuit, Wendy's improvement was dramatic. In 1969, when she began teaching, Wendy was ranked nineteenth in the United States. By the end of 1972, she was ranked fifth in the country, tenth in the world, was the eighth leading money winner on the Virginia Slims circuit, and, with partner Val Ziegenfuss, was the second-ranked doubles player in the United States. After a slip to tenth ranking in 1973, Wendy was again ranked in the top five in singles in 1975. Despite several arm ailments that limited her play in 1977 and 1978, Wendy was a finalist with Mary Carillo in the U.S. Clay Court doubles and a World Team Tennis player.

A slender 5 feet 9 inches, Wendy combines power and grace on the court. In this chapter she makes use of her experience as a teaching pro to make clear the basics of the backhand.

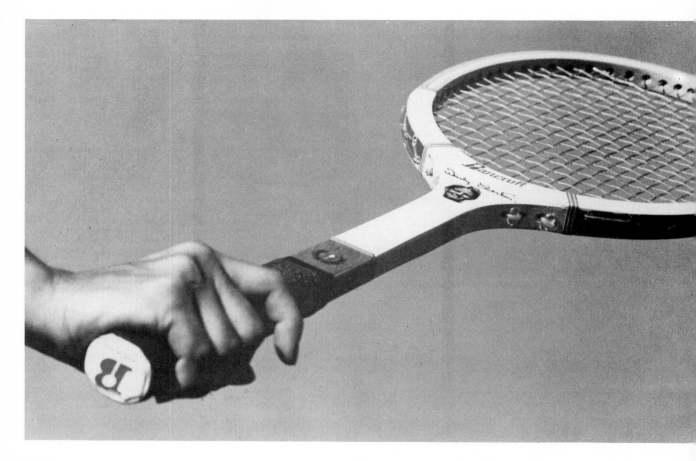

Although most beginners shy away from the backhand and find it awkward, the backhand is actually the easiest stroke in tennis. As a player matures, she usually finds that her backhand has become both stronger and more comfortable than her forehand. Because the backhand is one of the most basic and important strokes in tennis, I feel that it should be taught right at the very beginning, along with—not after—the forehand.

I was taught the backhand by Ed Faulkner—that is, he taught me to use the Eastern backhand grip. I had always used the Continental grip, but I found, with Ed's coaching, that I could get more power using the Eastern. To get the Eastern grip, hold the racket perpendicular to the ground and place the heel of your hand on the top of the racket handle. Now grip down firmly. The index finger should

be spread a bit more than the rest of the fingers, and the thumb should be slightly up the side of the racket handle. As a teaching pro, I teach the Eastern grip to my pupils. I'm sure there are a lot of people who disagree with me, a lot of people who prefer the Continental, but the Eastern works for me and I've seen it work for my pupils.

There are about a million different ways of hitting a given stroke and probably even a larger number of opinions as to how a given stroke should be taught. If you watch a pro tournament, you'll probably see that backhands are hit differently by almost every single competitor. While working as a teaching pro, I developed a simplified method of teaching the backhand. I believe you should learn the fundamentals early—the personal touches and philosophies can come later.

*I use the Eastern backhand grip. The index
finger is spread a little* (opposite), *the thumb is
slightly up the handle* (top left v. bottom
left), *and the hand is turned just a bit to your left
from the very top of the handle* (right).

Personally, I feel that my own backhand drive has improved greatly over the last couple of years simply by my having moved my thumb a little bit higher up the handle of the racket. I recommend that my students do the same. If four years ago someone had suggested to me that I should extend my thumb, I would have thought that he was crazy. But I was finally convinced to switch, and I feel that the change has added a lot of power to my stroke. Also, I discourage the hammer grip (fingers gripped closely together around the racket handle) because I think a player who uses it tends to lose the feel of the stroke.

I have learned a new, exciting philosophy in regard to stroke production. It aggressively contradicts old-school methods and would probably cause mild heart tremors among teaching professionals. However, I have found it more productive for my pupils if I use the most simplified teaching method. Before I start to teach a beginner how to stroke the ball, I impress on her the fact that there are three parts to any tennis stroke—the backswing, making contact with the ball, and the follow-through. Any time one of these ingredients is missing—if there are only two parts instead of three—it is not a stroke. There are a number of things you could call it but not a stroke.

For the right-hander, from a waiting position with the neck of the racket resting lightly in the left hand, begin a fluid backswing. The left hand helps take the racket back, and the right arm is fairly straight. Usually the back-

The stroke is composed of three parts. If any
one part is missing, it is no longer a stroke. From the
waiting position with the neck of the
racket resting lightly in the left hand (left), I begin
a fluid stroke. Backswing is not big.

swing will come to a level about even with the left hip. The weight is on the right leg, and the right foot is at a 45-degree angle to the net.

Keeping the right arm comfortably straight and the racket perpendicular to the ground—your right arm and the racket handle should form a 110-degree angle—swing straight through. It is very important to keep a firm wrist throughout the stroke. You should make contact with the ball at about waist height. The entire backhand stroke describes an arc of 180 degrees. The racket should make contact with the ball when you're a little more than halfway through your swing, or, say, when the racket is about six inches in front of your body.

The follow-through should continue through the ball and slightly upward, so that the racket winds up pointing toward the net and slightly up toward the sky. Throughout, your weight should be on your right foot.

Body position is very important. You should keep your right shoulder down and you should keep your head down. As you follow through, don't pull up. It's just as in golf—if you don't keep your head and shoulder down to the ball, if you pull up, then you're going to lose the ball and miss the shot.

There are several ways to hit a backhand —that is, there are several kinds of spin you can put on the ball. First of all, you have the flat backhand drive. The ball has no spin, and when it bounces on the other side of the court, it usually takes an even bounce.

If you bring your racket up and over the ball as you hit it, you'll hit a topspin, or overspin, backhand. The up-and-over motion puts a forward spin on the ball, giving it a sort of loopy trajectory. When the topspin drive bounces on the other side of the net, it hops, bouncing higher than does the flat drive.

The sliced backhand is exactly the opposite of the topspin shot. When executing a slice backhand, you approach the ball with the racket head slightly higher, hitting down and under the ball, causing the underspin.

I use all three shots when I'm rallying with my opponent from the backcourt. I use both the topspin and slice backhands for passing shots when my opponent is at net. I also find the slice backhand effective as an approach shot—the ball stays low in the air and takes a lower bounce. The slice is extremely effective on grass courts—on grass the ball doesn't seem to bounce at all.

I hit about an equal number of topspin backhands and slice backhands—I almost never hit a flat backhand. The reason for this is that I feel it's easier to control the ball with spin. I find that when I hit a flat shot, I can't be as precise with my placement as I can when I hit with spin, whether it be topspin or slice.

Very few of the top players in the game today do hit a flat backhand. Almost every competitor on the tour hits with either one spin or the other. Of course, the really versatile player is going to be able to hit all three types of backhand with proficiency.

The angle of my right foot (left) *is somewhat exaggerated, past the ideal angle of 45°. If it is not possible to hit the ball at waist level, bend down* (below). *Contact is made a bit out front, and the wrist–racket angle is 110°.*

There are a few players who hit the backhand stroke with two hands. I feel that learning the one-handed backhand is extremely important, especially if you want to play high-level tennis. (There are always exceptions to every rule—Chris Evert Lloyd and Cliff Drysdale are two notable exceptions.) The reason for this belief is simply that using a two-handed backhand cuts down reach to a large degree. A player who uses two hands on his backhand has to take two or three extra steps to get to the ball. In addition, it's very difficult to retrieve short-angle shots with it, and hitting those high, bouncing backhands is almost an impossibility. I would never encourage a two-handed backhand for the beginner. Of course, every person is different, with different levels of athletic prowess, and what might be best for one might be wrong for the other. All teachers should be flexible. I still maintain, however, that a weak one-handed backhand may limit your game somewhat in the beginning, but a two-handed backhand will limit you even more later on.

One of the most common mistakes made by beginners is jabbing at the ball. They tend to get their elbow out in front of their body, which causes an erratic, jabbing motion. Another problem beginners have is getting into the proper position. Most problems with the backhand can be corrected with a little bit of coaching and much practice and concentration.

One of the things I emphasize when teaching the backhand is keeping the racket arm fairly straight. This applies to the flat or topspin shot—on the slice backhand the arm is slightly bent and the racket face is slightly open. I do, however, think that you have to be flexible on every stroke. I drill my pupils during practice sessions to make them hit with a straight arm, but in practice or during an actual match, the arm is going to have to be bent from time to time. This isn't really a matter of "Do as I say, not as I do." It's a matter of learning the correct form. Once you have developed a good, basic form and your game has matured a little, you can afford to deviate from the rules every now and then.

I feel it's very important to see the ball hit the strings on every shot. Watching the ball come off the strings will in itself make you concentrate harder and will help you improve your strokes.

The basic difference between the way men players hit the backhand and the way women tennis players hit the backhand is power. The men simply hit the ball harder, and this is because they have larger, more powerful physiques. In the women's game, however, you don't have to have exceptional physical strength—power is timing. Again to use a golfing analogy, if you take a look at women golfers, you'll see that the tiniest lady golfer can drive the ball as far—well, perhaps almost as far—as the largest lady golfer. And why? Timing. You develop timing by hours of practice, by spending hours working on the fundamentals of the game.

*One of the most common mistakes made by
beginners is jabbing at the ball. They somehow feel
it is more natural to stick their elbows out
in front of their bodies, which of course causes many
problems, including the loss of pace.*

Opposed to the jabbing technique shown on the preceding pages, is the correct position (above.) *Many beginners also have problems hitting the high backhand, shown hit correctly* (right).

The ideal position from which to hit a backhand is one in which the ball is neither too far away from your body nor too close in. By forming the 110-degree angle with your arm and racket, you can determine how close you should be to the ball to be able to hit it without bending your elbow. As I've said, you should try to hit the ball at waist height and about six inches out in front of your body.

In attempting to execute a backhand drive, either flat or with topspin, many of my pupils start their backswings too high. If your backswing is too high, if the racket head is up around your shoulders, the end result will be a slice backhand every time. There's no way that you can hit a flat or a topspin backhand if your backswing is high. A common cause of a high backswing is a bent elbow. Remember to keep your arm straight and you'll be able to keep your backswing down where it belongs.

When hitting the slice backhand, I recommend that you take the ball on the rise. When executing the flat or topspin shot, hit the ball at waist level.

Many beginners have trouble hitting the high backhand. Especially when you're just starting out, I recommend that you just take two or three giant steps backward and then take the shot as a regular backhand drive rather than trying to hit the high backhand. You can, of course, in this situation, take the ball on the rise and hit the slice. I think it's easier, however, to get back, wait till the ball comes down, and hit the topspin or flat drive.

When you're playing at the net and your opponent lobs, she will almost invariably throw up the lob to your backhand side. This is one of the toughest shots in tennis, and it's a good shot to spend a lot of practice time on. During a match when this situation arises, I try to get back and play a high backhand volley. If the lob is hit very deep, then I'll let it bounce and hit a backhand lob—a topspin, if possible. Since the lob to your backhand is such a tough shot to get to, you'll find that hitting back a lob is the easiest thing to do. Also, of course, by putting up a lob, you give yourself time to get back into position.

Some players are very strong in this situation. Billie Jean King, for example, is renowned for this particular shot. If you hit

Rather than trying to execute the high,
slice backhand, it might be better for you to take
a couple of long steps back so that the ball
can be hit normally, at waist level.

a lob deep to her backhand corner, she'll scramble all the way back to behind the baseline, and then, at the very last moment, she'll flick the racket with her wrist and hit a beautiful backhand drive.

Another girl who has a very good backhand and a very strong wrist is Evonne Goolagong. It's very difficult to tell where Evonne is going to hit her backhand because, at the very last second, she can change its direction completely with a flick of her wrist.

As I said earlier, however, I don't use, or teach players to use, excess wrist in any shot. The wrist should be firm at all times. Evonne has a great shot, and I admire her for it, but I certainly wouldn't recommend that a beginner try to emulate her.

Normally the slice backhand is used to hit down the line, while the topspin backhand is used to hit cross-court. Of course, you can go either way with either shot, but these are the percentage shots.

The placement of your backhand is determined by where you meet the ball. If you're going to go cross-court, you hit the ball a little bit earlier. If you're going to go down the line, you wait a bit and hit the ball a little later. If you change your body position or realign your feet, you're going to give away your intentions to your opponent.

I try never to hit a backhand drive closer than 18 inches to the net—that is, I always try to leave a margin for error. This isn't a hard and fast rule. After you've allowed your-

self this margin for error, exactly how high you hit the ball over the net will be determined by your own style of play—how hard you hit the ball, what type of spin you use, and so on.

There is one drill that I feel has helped me a lot and which I strongly recommend, to beginners and to fairly advanced players as well. Find a partner who wants to practice the backhand. Place a racket cover at each end of the court and then trade backhand cross-courts and backhands down the line, all the time aiming for the racket covers. Once you get to the point that you can place the ball near the racket cover with a fair amount of consistency, you'll be able to hit your backhand with confidence during a match. By doing this simple drill every chance you get, you'll be surprised—and happy—at how quickly your backhand improves. There is no substitute for hard practice and concentration.

Joy Schwikert and I have placed racket covers in two corners of the court. We're practicing cross-court backhands by trying to hit the covers. It's a simple and effective drill.

The Forehand
by Valerie Ziegenfuss

Tennis should be a creative game, one of concepts, not checkpoints. The forehand is the perfect stroke with which to practice this philosophy.

Born in 1949, Valerie Ziegenfuss took up tennis 10 years later under the instruction of her father, a physical education teacher and basketball coach. "With two older brothers, I developed a competitive spirit at an early age. Fortunately my father recognized this and channeled my competitiveness into a useful area."

A graceful 5 feet 8 inches, 140 pounds, Valerie has represented the United States in Federation Cup play, as well as in the Bell Cup against Australia and the Wightman Cup against Great Britain. Winner of eight U.S. junior and three U.S. adult championships, Val has four times ranked in the U.S. top 10 in singles; she has twice been ranked number one in doubles.

A native of San Diego, California, Valerie learned tennis on fast surfaces and developed a potent serve-and-volley game. According to her, this is the major factor in her success as a doubles player. At the same time, however, she feels that the way in which she was taught has hampered her singles game. "In singles, the ground strokes—the forehand and the backhand—are important, and mine were all messed up."

Several years ago, Valerie was introduced to a new concept in ground strokes—actually in all strokes—that she feels has improved her game tremendously.

The forehand is, of course, one of the major parts of the game. It's the first stroke that most of us are introduced to, and it's the shot that we feel the most comfortable with early on. Strangely enough, though, the forehand is the stroke that gives many advanced players the most trouble. The reason for this is that the forehand is not as natural a movement across the body as is the backhand. Still, the forehand remains a very offensive stroke with which players attack and finish off the point. By the very nature of the shot being our "big weapon," players tend to miss more forehands than backhands because they try to do more things with it offensively and so, by taking more risks, lose some consistency and control.

A couple of years ago I met a man named Bill Glaves, from Houston, Texas, who changed my whole philosophy of hitting the ball. I come from California, where I was taught to hit basically flat shots because we play on very fast cement and there's no time to hit long loopy drives. My concept of how to hit a forehand consisted of several different thoughts. The steps to execute a forehand were (1) turn sideways to the net, (2) take the racket back quickly and low, (3) bend the knees and step into the shot with the left foot, (4) hit the ball in front and follow through out into the court. These instructions have been used for years to teach people the forehand and are still thought by most people to be the rule. I disagree with these teaching concepts. After trying Mr. Glaves's new ideas, I

can state, through experience, that forehands are a lot easier, and learned faster, when thought of in different and "new" concepts.

Before I describe the way I now hit the forehand, I want to explain the reasons for taking this different approach. First, I think instructors pay too much attention to detail. I'm after fluid strokes, not machinelike, step-by-step strokes. What I want to do is impart the concept, the overall picture, of hitting the forehand, not give a detailed, checkpoint-by-checkpoint blueprint. One of the most impor-

Though the forehand is the big weapon of most
players, it's the stroke with which they make
most mistakes. It's not natural
like the backhand because the follow-
through comes across the body, not away from it.

Tennis is a game of
concepts, and the
number-one concept is
that of putting
the ball back into
the court. It's
a little like the
concept of throwing.

tant aspects of tennis is flexibility. Every ball hit to you is a new experience; every ball is coming from a different angle at a different speed and is bouncing off a different part of the court surface. Every time you hit a tennis ball, you are faced with hundreds of variables. To me, it only makes sense that you should try to simplify your strokes rather than burden your mind with a lot of checkpoints. Understand the concept of putting the ball back into ͏posite court, and then do it in the manner ͏ost comfortable for you.

͏ you must keep your mind think- ͏d terms rather than getting ͏ied about elbows, shoul- ͏s, when you think ͏e to do with a ͏ple used to ͏sed that ͏ And

results rather than about detailed mechanics.

The first concept a beginner should grasp is that of getting the ball to move away from her body. I think of it as an "inside to outside" concept. The act of throwing a ball is an example. In order to throw the ball, the mind must first form the concept of an object, the ball, being moved away from the body. Now relate that to tennis in which the concept is the same but the hand is holding a racket. Your desire is for the racket head to make the ball go out. Because the mind wants the racket head to meet the ball, there will be contact, and because the mind is thinking "in to out," the ball will go away from the body.

Now a second concept, that of "outside to inside," must be added to the first. In other words, the ball is going to be coming at you (out to in) and you are going to want to direct the ball back (in to out). Once the beginner is aware that these are the two principal concepts the mind will have to deal with, we can pro- ͏d with actually how to get the ball back ͏ the net.

͏he way in which the ball goes over the ͏cally, a matter of the laws of phys- ͏se laws are followed, the shot will ͏ssful; that is, the ball *will* go over the ͏ is necessary, first, to see the ball in its ͏ path rather than as a single object. The ͏th that the ball creates from the moment it ͏strikes your opponent's racket to the moment it strikes yours is the "line of flight." It is this line of flight that the racket head must counter

43

The racket head must counter the line of flight
in order to get the ball back into the court.

tant aspects of tennis is flexibility. Every ball hit to you is a new experience; every ball is coming from a different angle at a different speed and is bouncing off a different part of the court surface. Every time you hit a tennis ball, you are faced with hundreds of variables. To me, it only makes sense that you should try to simplify your strokes rather than burden your mind with a lot of checkpoints. Understand the concept of putting the ball back into the opposite court, and then do it in the manner that is most comfortable for you.

I believe you must keep your mind thinking in generalized terms rather than getting too specific and worried about elbows, shoulders, and knees. Besides, when you think about it, what do knees have to do with a racket hitting a flying object! People used to tell me, "Valerie, the reason you missed that shot is that you didn't bend your knees." And I'd listen to them and concentrate on bending my knees. The trouble was that I started missing shots because my mind was thinking "knees" instead of "ball over net." It really makes me mad now to think about all that wasted time and effort I spent worrying about my knees. You just don't *have* to bend your knees to hit low shots. I say you don't have to, but if you feel more comfortable bending your knees, if that's the way you feel you hit the shot best, then by all means do so. All I'm saying is don't overload your mind with a lot of useless details. Keep the end in mind, not the means. Get the brain thinking about end

results rather than about detailed mechanics.

The first concept a beginner should grasp is that of getting the ball to move away from her body. I think of it as an "inside to outside" concept. The act of throwing a ball is an example. In order to throw the ball, the mind must first form the concept of an object, the ball, being moved away from the body. Now relate that to tennis in which the concept is the same but the hand is holding a racket. Your desire is for the racket head to make the ball go out. Because the mind wants the racket head to meet the ball, there will be contact, and because the mind is thinking "in to out," the ball will go away from the body.

Now a second concept, that of "outside to inside," must be added to the first. In other words, the ball is going to be coming at you (out to in) and you are going to want to direct the ball back (in to out). Once the beginner is aware that these are the two principal concepts the mind will have to deal with, we can proceed with actually how to get the ball back over the net.

The way in which the ball goes over the net is, basically, a matter of the laws of physics. If those laws are followed, the shot will be successful; that is, the ball *will* go over the net. It is necessary, first, to see the ball in its full path rather than as a single object. The path that the ball creates from the moment it strikes your opponent's racket to the moment it strikes yours is the "line of flight." It is this line of flight that the racket head must counter

*The racket head must counter the line of flight
in order to get the ball back into the court.*

in order to make the incoming ball go back out into the court. For instance, if the line of flight is coming down and the stroke is coming up, then the ball will go off the racket head at an upward angle. If the stroke is level, the ball will travel off the racket head at a downward angle (see diagram).

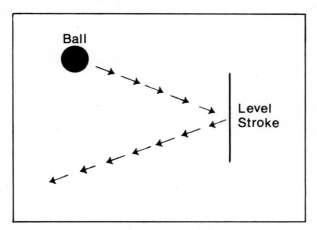

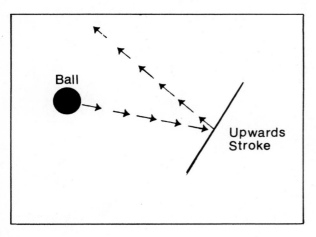

Finding the correct angle for the face of the racket in order to determine the correct line of flight is a matter of trial and error. Finding the correct line should, however, always be done with the total concept in mind. You will also discover that the wrist must be in a position of strength to help control the ball during contact.

The next concept to learn is one of hand–eye coordination. The pressure created by the ball against the racket head has a very identifiable feel. When the racket head comes through the ball fast, there is not as much pressure on the strings for you to feel as there would be were the ball to remain on the strings a longer time, which would create more pressure for a better feel. It is this "feel of the ball" that you need to learn and develop for control.

Once you grasp the actual physical aspects of tennis, you must understand some concepts of development. The most important thing to do when developing any skill is to implant an end result in your mind. Learning consists of placing the end result in your mind and allowing the brain to attempt the action to bring that result. That result is then compared with other results so that in the future the mind has enough comparisons to ensure a higher percentage of successful shots. The simplest example of this procedure is a child learning to stand. First, the child makes the attempt to balance himself but falls to one side. With that experience the child tries again

and falls the other way. Eventually the child stands straight, managing to keep from falling to one side or the other. When you relate this experience to tennis, you find that the brain may experience first the feel of going too short with the ball and then the feel of going too long, but eventually, with experience, the brain recognizes the correct distance by retaining the positive experiences and rejecting the negative responses. So, it is because of the experiences of hitting the ball against the back fence and into the bottom of the net that eventually you are able to hit the ball into the court.

Once the brain has experienced enough forehands and is able to produce a basic stroke, you are ready for the next step. In order to understand advanced concepts of the forehand, you must have advanced thoughts. Your first concept was very broad, that concept being the "court." Now you have a more refined end thought, which is an actual ball over net to court. Then you advance the ball over net to *corner* of court. Next you start thinking "ball over net to corner *fast.*" Finally, at a very advanced stage, you are able to think "ball over net fast to *spot!*"

By now you've developed the basic forehand stroke and are able to do something with the ball. But let's not be naïve about our ever-changing problem at hand. You have developed a high degree of mental feel for a ball going out; in other words, the in-coming ball has been a simple shot about which you've been thinking advanced ends. In order to develop your hand–eye coordination even further, you must complicate the concept of the ball coming in to you. You find yourself having to adjust to new variables, and as a result you find yourself unable to do as much with the ball as you once were able to do. Example: The winner of a ladies' club tournament enters a Virginia Slims tournament and discovers the level of play to be higher. She plays all the same shots she normally hits against the club members, but she misses them all against the professional player. She comes off the court feeling disgusted with herself for playing so badly, when in truth, her opponent made her miss because the incoming ball was hit that much more aggressively and was designed to make her miss. Her mistake was in still trying to do so much with her shots and in not recognizing all the existing variables created when the better player hit a little harder or placed her shots in more difficult spots than the club players had.

Now you can understand the reason that people become fanatics on this game. No matter how many shots you can hit, there's always a new challenge ahead of you. It's this learning to adjust to the variables that makes the game so fascinating. Taking it to the ultimate, just imagine returning an overhead smash hit by John Newcombe at 100 miles an hour in the form of a topspin lob hit on the run. The ball arches over Newk's left shoulder and bounces on the line for a winner! Wow, wouldn't that be an all-timer!

I use a shake-hands grip and keep my hand fairly close to my body. The complete swing often starts with a small loop. The racket starts high (top right), comes under the ball (middle right), and then goes up and over in a follow-through (bottom right) that imparts topspin.

Let me try to summarize the way I now hit the forehand. First of all, I use the Eastern grip—the "shake-hands" grip—which I think is the most widely used grip. (For a more formal discussion on grips, refer to either Kerry Reid or Rosemary Casals.) Next, I try to keep my hands close to my body because hitting is more comfortable and easier when it is done within the working area of my body. I don't want to be bothered thinking about all the little checkpoints—stepping with the left foot, getting the body sideways to the net and so on. As I start the swing, I concentrate on the relationship of my hand to the ball and on working the ball back out into the target area. On contact, there is a split second when I am not looking at the ball. The brain has already computed the trajectory of the ball, and I have already initiated the swing in a plane that ensures contact with the ball. In fact, the split second that you are not looking at the ball should occur when the ball is already on the strings.

A lot of people will say that you should never take your eyes off the ball, that you should watch the ball hit the strings. Well, first of all you have to hit the ball over a barrier—the net—and then you have to hit the ball into a confined area. If your eyes never leave the ball, there's no way for your brain to think the end result. So for just the tiniest fraction of a second, the moment that the ball is on the strings, your eyes will be on the target area.

Another point of contention is the point at which the racket should meet the ball. I always wait and let the ball come in to me. Many people will say that you should meet the ball out in front of your body. I think that this is confusing because the ball should be *released* in front. The follow-through does the work, and if the ball is met too far in front, the swing will be completed and there will be no follow-through left and no place to go. I like for beginners to hit the ball close enough to themselves so that there is maximum power but not close enough to cause them a cramped backswing.

How do you get power and where does it come from? A general concept in sports is that the majority of power is produced through the body. The teaching pro tells the pupil to get her weight going forward into the ball. This may sound solid, but does adding mass add power? Let's examine the formula for kinetic energy. It is $KE = \frac{1}{2}mv^2$. The three components are energy, mass, and velocity. Applying this formula, you discover that you can achieve greater power by increasing the velocity of the racket head through the ball rather than by throwing extra body weight (mass) into the ball. For example, take a golf tee and place it on your hand. Hit it with your fist. That represents mass times mass, and the tee goes only a short distance. Now take the tee in your hand and snap it away with your finger. That represents mass times velocity, and the tee probably flew halfway across the room!

All this means is that the racket head must generate the power and must be allowed to come through the ball completely in order to gain the most control and power. If I lean forward to a degree that lessens racket head speed, I will lose power, whereas if I have to hit the ball falling away but still generate racket head speed into it, I won't lose power.

All players have been seen hitting off the wrong foot. Yet they still generate power and look fluent. This is not to say that you should fall away and hit off the wrong foot, but as long as there is a complete follow-through working, the rest is secondary.

I purposely have not described my fore-

I let the ball come in to me, rather than trying to hit it too far out front. A strong follow-through does the work. Hit the ball close enough for power, but avoid a cramped backswing.

My body is in an open stance, my arm is bent, my elbow is close to my body.

hand in the normal checkpoint terms because I *never* think about my stroke in those terms. For those who still need such an explanation, my forehand would look like this. My body is in an open stance, my arm is bent, my elbow is close to my body, and my wrist is squared off to the ball. I hit the ball on the inside, which adds power and control. The racket comes up over the ball to impart topspin, and the follow-through is to the inside of the ball. In the follow-through the body follows the arm. That is, if you are pulling through the ball hard enough, the force of the follow-through should cause your body to torque. Remember, this is a description of what happens as a spectator sees it; I *never* think in those terms. I think that the most important thought I have in my mind when chasing a ball is to *put* the ball back out into the court.

For beginning players it is best not to get into the techniques of my swing because those techniques are brought about by my mind's thinking about the end result of what I want to accomplish. The mind is consciously able to think about only three concepts per second; the preconscious mind can handle thousands. Therefore, I must allow my preconscious mind

My wrist is squared off to the ball (opposite top). *On the follow-through, I pull hard enough through the ball so that my body twists* (right).

54

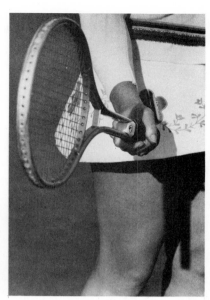

to do more work by giving the conscious mind concepts of a broad nature—concepts such as "where" I want the ball to go rather than of "how" I want my body to move.

People often ask me to describe special techniques I use for stroke production; that is, how do I hit cross-court or down the line. These are pitfalls I try to avoid because as soon as I become more aware of body techniques, my mind loses the total awareness of the shot. Because I adapt to the variables, I appear to be more fluent, avoiding rigidity

caused by my mind's inability to deal with too many conscious concepts.

When trying to hit cross-court, I place in my mind the end result: "cross-court." From there the mind will take care of meeting the ball a fraction of a second early to send the ball cross-court. Similarly, with the shot down the line, I must have in my mind a mental image of the end result before the mind can make the judgment to meet the ball a fraction of a second late to send it down the line.

I almost always hit a topspin forehand.

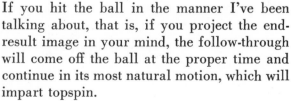

If you hit the ball in the manner I've been talking about, that is, if you project the end-result image in your mind, the follow-through will come off the ball at the proper time and continue in its most natural motion, which will impart topspin.

As long as I'm hitting the ball with top-spin, I don't want to flirt with the lines. My ball will be moving forward because of the topspin, which means that my opponent will be unable to do anything overly aggressive with it because it is moving on her. Shots that

How do I hit cross-court or down the line? I think "cross-court" or "down the line." From the same position and with the same stroke, it's easy to go either cross-court (opposite left and right) or down the line (above).

fall short in the court but are hit with power can't be classified as shallow. Short shots hit without speed will be taken advantage of, but when you start hitting balls that are in by inches, before long you are going to start hitting balls that are out by inches. And since I attempt to play points in a manner that allows the highest percentage of winning them, I would never aim *for* a line but rather *inside* a line where I have a margin for error.

There was a time when almost every forehand I hit was flat or, in other words, had no spin at all. This was before I was introduced to the new concepts I've been talking about and while I was still hitting according to the old rules—racket straight back, racket straight through the ball with the follow-through out into the court. As a result of this approach, I was a very erratic player. I just didn't have the ball control that I've since developed. Perhaps the most important factor here is the point I've already made about the follow-through that keeps the ball from sailing out of the court. This follow-through, which controls the ball, is caused by having the mental image of wanting the ball to dip after it has cleared the net.

Most of the top players use the topspin forehand. It's the easiest shot to control and it's an aggressive shot. I haven't talked about the slice, or undercut, forehand mainly because I don't like that shot as much as the topspin. The underspin is a definite part of the game, though, because when the ball is *put* back out into the desired spot, certain situa-

*Although this seems to be a standard
backswing (left), as far as I'm concerned it's all
wrong. The arm is straight, the wrist is not
squared, and the racket is too far back. My arm
is close to my body (above left),* and my wrist
is squared (above right), *yet I easily reach the ball.*

In this case the ball has come in close and I haven't had time to get into ideal position, but using the same stroke as always, I hit just the way I want, with a real strong follow-through.

tions call for the body to respond with certain kinds of shots. For example, Margaret Court uses the undercut forehand for her down-the-line approach shot as a counter shot to a cross-court forehand hit by her opponent. She does this because it is the easiest way to put the ball back low and fast to that corner off that difficult shot.

A great advantage to having all the different shots is that you can change pace and depth. I think that the change of depth is most often the cause for lost points among women players. Most of the girls move quite well laterally, but for some reason they don't seem to move up and back very well. Also, players misread the pace of the ball as it comes over the net, an error that breaks their rhythm and throws them off stride.

It's often necessary to adapt your stroke to the kind of surface you're playing on. On fast surfaces, such as grass, where the ball stays low, you must think of the ball as having a lower trajectory back out into the target area. On slow surfaces, such as clay, you have more time to hit the ball. The court, because of the increased angles caused by the slower bounces, seems much larger. On clay, you can loop the ball more and allow wider shots to be hit.

Once again, I'd like to emphasize the importance of having the overall picture as opposed to worrying about a lot of details. You should be aware of what is happening on the court, at both ends, rather than being inside yourself, trying to remember checkpoints. I think that over the years tennis instructors have put too much emphasis on the negative—"don't do this" and "don't do that." Putting restrictions on a beginning player only confuses her and causes her to tighten up.

Tennis is a very complicated game, but it should be fun. It is, after all, a game. And since tennis is a difficult game to master, I think that it should be taught in a simple, log-

ical way. If you just remember the basic concept of putting the ball back out into its line of flight and stop worrying about the "don'ts," you will be able to relax and enjoy the game. Most important of all, realize, even before you think about picking up a racket, that your mind is an excellent computer that will continue to develop if you let it and don't fight it.

I feel that Mr. Glaves has opened up a whole new world for me. I know that my game is progressing every day, and I truly believe that some day his concepts will be the rule instead of the new idea. I hope that you will try thinking along these same lines because it has brought me nothing but pleasure and freedom to create on the court—and that to me, fellow players, is what it is all about. Happy creating with your "big weapon!"

The Serve and the Return of Serve

by Lesley Hunt

If you never lose your serve, you'll never lose
a match. The serve, while so important, is probably
the most difficult shot in tennis.

Born in Perth, Australia, in 1950, Lesley Hunt took up tennis at the age of 10 at her father's urging, "Mainly because I was demolishing the house and he wanted to tire me out." By age 14 she was state champion of Western Australia, and by age 17 she was Australian Junior champion, a title she won three times.

In 1969, at the age of 18, Lesley made her presence known to the tennis world by defeating Judy Dalton and Ann Jones. She has four times reached the quarterfinals of the U.S. Open and has scored victories over such players as Rosemary Casals, Kerry Reid, Françoise Dürr, Wendy Overton, and Betty Stöve.

Although Lesley has always been blessed with exceptional ability and stamina, her main problem has been inconsistency. To remedy it, she took time off from the tour to take instruction from Pancho Segura, who not only coached her in overall tactics, but gave her pointers on improving concentration, especially on the big points.

Lesley married Jim Hambuechen in 1976 and underwent surgery to correct a torn tendon in her elbow in 1977. Since then, she has been coming back in a big way. She won the Swiss Championships at Gstaad in 1977; she began 1978 with a semifinal result at Avon of San Carlos and a win over Terry Holladay on the Virginia Slims Tour, then was twice a singles quarterfinalist, three times a doubles semifinalist, and a doubles finalist at the U.S. Indoors on the Colgate Series tour. In 1979, she won three doubles events with teammate Sharon Walsh.

In tennis, at any level, you will serve about 50 percent of the games played. If you never lose your serve, you're not going to lose the match. For this reason, the serve is certainly one of the most, if not the most, important shots in the game. You initiate each point with the serve, and the more forceful, the more accurate, your serve is, the more you're going to put your opponent on the defensive.

The serve is a sort of throwing action, so the best way to begin to learn it is by throwing. Stand on the baseline and practice throwing the ball, either a real or imaginary one, into the service court. This throwing action is basic to the serve, and it's one of the most difficult movements to learn, especially for a girl.

When I first started playing tennis, I did a lot of swinging without the ball. This is an exercise that I think does a lot of good for the beginner. Using two rackets, start the swing downward, bring it up behind your head in what we call in Australia the Indian club swing—your hand should be behind your head and the top of the heads of the rackets should be pointing toward the ground—then swing forward with your arm fully extended, follow through down on your right side, and repeat the entire process without stopping. You will follow through on your left side when you serve in actual play, but for the purpose of continued motion in this exercise, follow through on the right and continue into the next club swing. I used to do this exercise 50 times a day. Then, when I went on the court and

As a beginner I practiced the Indian club swing, which I found the easiest way to learn the serving motion. Use two rackets, and make each serve flow—one motion into the next.

actually tried to hit the serve, I concentrated on using the exact same motion that I had used in my practice sessions. This exercise helps to develop both limberness and strength.

The grip that I use and recommend for the serve is the Continental. To get this grip, hold the racket as though you were shaking hands with it. Now move your hand a quarter-turn to the left, if you're right-handed. Keep the fingers of the racket hand together—don't spread them too much or place the index finger up the handle. The heel of your hand should be against the heel of the racket. If you "choke" the racket by holding it too far up the handle, you will limit the full flexibility of your wrist.

When preparing to serve, you should stand about a yard or a yard and a half to either side of the center line. The set position for the serve should be the most relaxed position you can find. Your feet should be about two feet or so apart—whatever is most comfortable for you. Position your feet so that the line from the toe of the back foot to the toe of the front foot points to the spot to which you want the ball to go. You can check this by standing the racket on edge on the ground across the front of your feet so that it touches the toes of both feet. The racket head should point to your target.

Again, the idea once you get on the court is to keep intact the swing you've practiced. In order to do this, you must throw the ball up to a spot where your racket will make

I use the Continental grip when serving. Grasp the racket handle as if you're shaking hands with it, then move your hand a quarter-turn counterclockwise. Keep your fingers fairly close to each other, including the index finger.

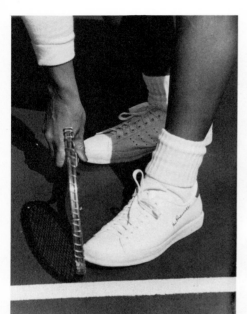

*Position your feet so that the
line from the toe of the back
shoe to the toe of the front shoe
points where you want the
ball to go. Check it by standing
the racket on edge on the ground
across the front of your feet.*

contact with the ball without your having to vary your swing.

There are three basic kinds of serves: the flat serve, the spin serve, and the kicker, or American twist, serve. For each of these serves, the ball has to be thrown up to a slightly different spot.

The flat serve is the power serve. It has no spin on it to speak of, and it's the serve that almost all players use for their first serve. If you hope to develop into a competitive player, you'll have to be able to serve and volley, at least some of the time. And to be able to serve and volley to full advantage, you'll need to be able to hit the flat serve.

To throw the ball up for the flat serve, imagine that you're facing a large clock, then throw the ball up to the spot where one o'clock would be. This should place the ball directly in the arc of the swing you've been practicing. If you let the ball fall to the ground, it should bounce about a foot in front of and a little to the right of your forward foot, which is the left foot if you're right-handed. You may want to experiment with just how far you toss the ball in front of you. Generally speaking, the farther forward you throw the ball, the harder you will be able to hit it and the better trajectory you will get. It will depend on your reach and your timing. If, on the other hand, you toss the ball too close to you and still hit it hard, you'll find your serves going long.

Once you have worked enough with the racket to know how high you need to toss the

The flat serve is hit with no spin.
The racket makes contact with the ball dead center and does not come across the ball.

*For the flat serve, throw the ball up to
a point that could be one o'clock were you facing a
clock (opposite). In the spin serve (below),
the ball is farther to the right and the racket comes
around the ball to impart sidespin.*

ball, practice the throw-up without hitting. Just toss the ball up and let it fall to the ground. Watch to see that it's striking in the right spot—a foot in front of and a little to the right of your left foot. This is a drill you should spend a lot of time on if you want to develop a good serve.

For the spin serve—the serve that most women players use for the second serve—the tossup is basically the same except that the ball should be thrown a little more out to the right and not as far forward as for the first serve. Again imagine the clock face, but this time aim the ball for the spot that would be two o'clock. The stroke on the spin serve is also basically the same—the basic throwing action, or Indian club swing—except that since the ball is farther out to your right, you have to come around the ball more and hit it more or less on its outside edge. Coming around the ball imparts sidespin to the ball and causes it to "go off" as it hits the service court. The spinner serve goes off to your left, your opponent's right, after bouncing.

For the kicker, or American twist, serve, aim your tossup at twelve o'clock on the imaginary clock. The ball should also be thrown farther back over your head. In this case, if you let the ball bounce, it should hit about six inches to the left of your left foot and about on a level with it. Since you're throwing the ball back over your head, you'll have to exaggerate the arch in your back for this serve. The racket face comes up under the

I don't recommend the kicker serve to anyone
without a nimble back, and that includes myself. Mona
Schallau (below) *demonstrates the correct kicker.*
The ball is thrown to twelve o'clock, back arch is
exaggerated, and the racket comes around the ball in
a direction opposite from the way it does with the spinner.

ball and then over and around it in a direction opposite to that used for the spin serve. It's like throwing a screwball in baseball. The spin imparted to the ball by this motion causes the ball to kick away from the receiver after it has bounced. The kicker serve kicks to your right, your opponent's left, after bouncing.

As you begin the service action, your weight should be evenly distributed. Then, as you start to toss up the ball and begin to take your racket back, your weight should transfer to the back (right) foot. Be sure to look at the ball as you throw it up, and keep your eyes on it until the moment of impact. The racket arm should be at a comfortably full stretch as it goes down into the backswing—the racket shouldn't quite touch the ground, but it should be held at a comfortable arm's length.

As the racket begins to come up into the Indian club position, your body should begin to move forward. Remember that in the Indian club position, the top of the racket head should be pointing at the ground behind you. As the racket starts up from the Indian club position toward the ball, your weight should be coming forward onto your left foot and your right foot should be moving up toward your left foot. Some players bring their right foot next to their left and hit the serve with their feet together. Others hit it with the right foot brought only halfway toward the left. It's just a matter of finding what works best for you. In any case, all your weight should come through together on the ball. If you've thrown

As you begin the service motion, your weight
should be evenly distributed and the racket arm
should be at a comfortably full stretch as
it goes down into the backswing (opposite). As the
racket begins to come into the Indian
club position, your body begins to move
forward (above). Your right foot moves up to the left.

The serve is a continuous motion throughout, including the follow-through, which brings the racket down to the left, across your body. The grip should be firm but the wrist loose (left) *until the moment of contact* (above).

the ball correctly, there should be no break at all in the movement. The serve should be one smooth, continuous motion from start to finish.

After you've hit the serve, your follow-through should bring the racket down on your left side. When hitting the kicker serve, some people bring the racket down on their right-hand side. This helps to impart extra spin to the ball, giving it added snap. However, this is a maneuver that requires an exceptionally strong wrist and back. I personally don't do it, and I don't really recommend it to most women players.

While we're talking about wrists, let me point out that the serve is unlike most other shots in tennis in that the wrist is never locked. The more fluid your wrist action, the better your serve will be. You should keep a firm grip on your racket, but the wrist should be loose until the moment of contact. At that moment it should snap over. The stronger your wrist, the harder the snap will be. Most of the power, however, comes from timing. The pace of the serve comes from a triple whip action—the whip of your back, shoulder, and wrist, hopefully all coming together at the same impact point. If your tossup is in the correct spot, if your service action is smooth and continuous, and if you hit the ball in the center of the racket face, you will have power.

During the service action, your left shoulder should be pointing at the spot to which you're serving the ball. In fact, your shoulders should be parallel to the line that

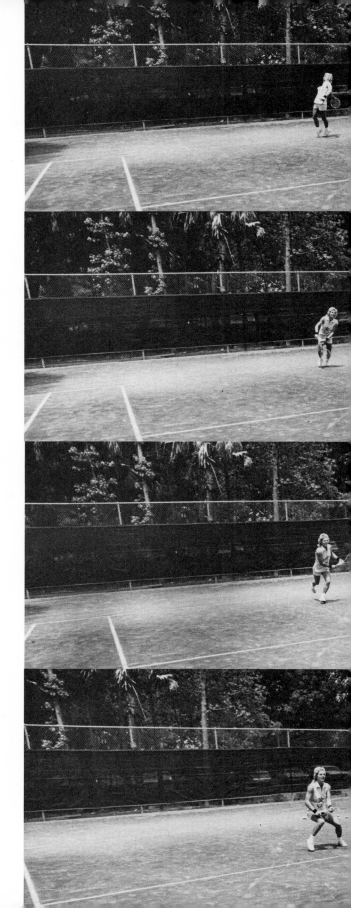

your feet form. Your shoulders should not start to swing around until the moment that you begin to bring your back foot forward. If your shoulders start forward too soon, the continuity of your serve will be broken and your head will turn, forcing your eyes away from the ball.

As I pointed out at the beginning, if you want to play a serve and volley game, then you must develop a good flat first serve. The flat serve almost compels you to go to the net, since if you don't step forward after you hit it, you're likely to fall on your face. Once you've taken that first step, you may as well keep going. In the basic serve and volley technique, the flat serve to the backhand in either service court is the best serve.

The type of serve you hit and where you hit it affects the way you come in to the net. If, for example, you're serving into the deuce court and you serve a flat serve to the backhand, then you should come in to the center of the court, straddling the center service line, and hit your first volley from there. If you're serving to the ad court and you serve a flat serve wide to the backhand, then you must come in to the net on your forehand, or right, side to protect your line. If you serve wide to the forehand in the deuce court, then you must come in to the left of the center line. Any time you serve down the center line, you should come in to the center of the net, straddling the center line.

No matter what kind of serve I hit in a

*Any time you serve down the center line, you
should come to the center of the net,
straddling the center service line, and hit
your first volley from there. I've
done just that* (left) *after serving to the ad court.*

*Here I've served to the deuce court, wide
to my right-handed opponent's forehand. In order
to protect the angle, I come in on a line,
to my left of the center service line, and volley.*

serve-and-volley situation, I try to get as close to the net as possible. I feel that the closer to the net you are, the greater your advantage. Hopefully, the first volley you hit will be a kill-off. If you're not quite quick enough to get in to put away the first volley, it should at least be well placed, into a deep corner. If you hit the first volley short and don't make a winner of it, then you're left open on both flanks. This calls for a split-second decision. As you come to net, you must decide whether you can put away the first volley or whether you should use it to set up a winner on the next shot.

If you are hitting your serve solidly and confidently, you should always take the advantage and follow it to the net. If, on the other hand, you are hitting the serve short and your opponent is getting a good line on the ball, then stay back, play from the baseline, and wait for a chance to hit an approach shot before going to net.

It's important to find the serve that suits your game. If you want to play serve and volley, then it's almost imperative that you develop a flat first serve. If you prefer to play your points from the baseline, then the flat first serve is possibly not the best serve for you. For one thing, as I've pointed out, the flat serve forces you to take that first step toward the net. If you're not going to follow the serve to the net, there's no point in taking that first step forward and then jumping back again. Also, the flat first serve takes a lot of effort and can be very tiring. You've really got to have the killing volley, the short rallies, to be able to use it consistently.

If you don't have a good net game or if you prefer playing your points from the baseline, then the best thing to do is to develop a good spin serve. If you're going to play from the baseline, then you're going to have longer rallies and you're going to hit a lot of drives. Using the spin serve will conserve energy and

will keep you in place on the baseline. The American twist serve will do essentially the same thing, but I think that for a woman the spin serve is easier.

It's also important to be able to vary your serve. The reason for this is that if you serve the ball at the same speed to the same spot time after time, it's likely that your opponent will get into a groove and begin to be successful with her returns. Of course, if you're serving

well, getting to the net, and winning your service games easily, then there's no point in changing—never change a winning game. But if you're missing your first serve or if your opponent is stepping in on it and making consistently good returns, varying your serve will give you a chance to unsettle her rhythm.

Perhaps you've decided that your opponent's biggest weakness is her forehand and you've served consistently to that side. She is

Standing on the wrong side of the center line is a foot fault. My back foot is in a fault position (right) *before I've even begun to serve.*

becoming used to the serve to her forehand and is getting into a rhythm with her returns. Now's the time to change and serve a few to her backhand. You can always go back to serving to the forehand once you've broken her rhythm. You can also vary the depth of your serve, although basically the best service is deep. In the case of a heavily angled serve, however, such as a spin serve wide in the deuce court to your opponent's forehand, the shorter the serve the better. That creates a sharper angle and forces your opponent to run not only wide to get to the ball but also forward, making her run even farther if your next shot is to her backhand corner. Some players find it easier to stand right over at the alley to serve a really wide angle. Two problems arise if you do that. First, you have alerted your opponent to your intention, and second, *you* have a lot of ground to cover if she hits it down your backhand lane.

Thus far I haven't said anything about aces. The reason for this is that aces come about almost accidentally. They happen when you're trying to hit a hard first serve to get you to the net. You're pushing on the serve, trying to put your opponent on the defensive so that she'll hit you up an easy volley. Occasionally in this situation, your opponent will miss the ball completely, and you've got an ace. It's nice when it happens, but don't be upset when it doesn't. You see more aces in men's tennis than you do in women's tennis simply because the men are stronger and have

greater reach—but not one of them can guarantee an ace every time he tries for it. I think that most good women players are not going to waste their energy trying for aces. They're going to save their strength for the game—net rushing or rallying from the baseline—rather than risk their strength on something that may not be wholly productive. Women are more likely to serve for accuracy—to open up the court for the second shot.

The definition of a foot fault has varied a great deal in the last decade—in the entire

I start out correctly (left), *but then swing my back foot into the wrong side,* (below).

history of tennis, for that matter. There are, at the present time, two common foot faults. One is standing on the wrong side of the center mark on the baseline. A lot of players foot fault in this manner by accident, as a result of crowding the center mark. They'll place their forward foot correctly next to the T formed by the center mark and the baseline, but then the back foot is not in line with the front and is actually on the wrong side of the center mark. Foot fault.

Stepping on the baseline or into the court

Stepping on the line with either foot before hitting the ball is another foot fault.
I step onto the line with my forward foot (left),
and I hit the line with my back foot (below).

with either foot before making contact with the ball is the other common foot fault. It's permitted to break the plane of the baseline, for instance, by swinging your right foot over into the court, but if it touches the ground before the ball is hit, then that is a foot fault.

At one time, a player was not allowed to "walk" during the service action. This meant that the front foot had to remain stationary during the serve. This rule, however, no longer applies, and nowadays you'll see a number of players—Wendy Overton, for example—who step first with the forward foot, then with the back foot.

You should be able to feel, if you're conscious of what you're doing during the serve, the position of your feet. During one period, I was consistently committing foot faults by bringing my back foot too far forward, past my front foot, and placing it on the line. To solve this problem, I placed a brick on the baseline and practiced my serve. After I had kicked the brick enough times with my right foot, I finally developed a feel for the baseline —not to mention a sore toe.

Personally, I prefer to stand four to six inches behind the baseline. A lot of players like to stand closer than this, to place their forward foot right next to the line. If, however, you are prone to creeping or turning your foot —some players keep their toe firmly planted but manage somehow to turn their heel all the way around onto the line—then you're better off to stand a bit back from the line.

A lot of weekend players do foot fault. One reason for this is, perhaps, that they have no official to call them for it. If you do foot fault, however, you're actually penalizing yourself. A lot of people seem to think that foot faulting gives an added advantage—you can get to the net faster, the ball has less distance to travel, and so on. Although it's conceivable that you might make it to the net a fraction sooner, there are more disadvantages to foot faulting than advantages. In order to foot fault, you have to break the line of your feet, your shoulders, and the service swing itself. By breaking this line, you force yourself to adjust your swing in mid-serve. This adjustment breaks your rhythm, which in turn costs you both power and accuracy. The more correctly you can serve, the better it is for your service. And you'll get to the net, if that's where you're going, just as fast—faster, in fact, having retained your balance.

The stage of the game—the score, in other words—will also affect the way you serve. If you are ahead by some games, you might like to try for a big ace at 15–all; or a wide slice serve to the forehand at 40–15. At tighter stages, such as 30–all, you should stick to sound, basic play. If I were serving at 30–all, I'd probably serve a medium-paced first serve to the backhand to be sure of getting it in, rather than a big one, and follow it to the net. I'm not advocating this particular play for everyone, but you should play something you feel comfortable and confident with. If I'm serving at 40–30, I'm going to get my first serve in deep to the backhand—again a medium-paced ball. Remember in these situations that your opponent is under pressure, too. Get your first serve in—the deeper it is, the more pressure you'll put on her.

It's handy to keep in the back of your mind that some players can return a hard serve better than they can a soft one. If you're serving hard and well but your opponent is still hitting good returns, you might be wise to try hitting a softer, loopier serve that will bounce higher. This puts pressure on your opponent to make something of the return rather than just making use of your pace.

The best service usually is the one that is deep in the service court, either to the backhand or forehand. There are players, however, who prefer to reach and who can hit the ball at very sharp angles by doing so. When you are up against this kind of opponent, you should try serving to the deep middle of the service court—or, in other words, directly at your opponent's body. This is a situation in which the kicker serve is very handy. If you can serve to your opponent's forehand and make the ball then kick into her body, you'll usually find that she has a great deal of trouble making a decent return.

Many beginners are in doubt as to how hard they should hit their second serve. Basically I would say that the second serve should be hit at about one-half or three-quarters the pace of the first serve. It really is impossible,

One way to prevent yourself from swinging your back
foot onto the line or into the court before
you hit the ball is to put something like a brick
on the service line. After bruising
your toes a few times, you should be cured.

though, to prescribe this kind of thing for another person. Each player must find her own pace. If you hit a flat first serve and a spin second serve, then naturally the second will be a good deal softer, since you can't—and shouldn't—hit a spin serve with the same power you would use on a flat serve. A good rule to follow, I would think, is to hit the second serve as hard as you possibly can and still be confident that the ball will go into the service court.

There is really very little reason to double-fault. If you've practiced your serve sufficiently, you should be able to hit the second serve with confidence every time. This is especially true if you use a spinner for the second serve. Double faults occur more frequently when the game gets tight and the pressure is all on your ability to get that second serve in. The best thing to do then is to serve a slower first serve and be sure to get that one in, instead of putting all that pressure on the second serve.

Once again, it's important to find the serve that suits your game. In some cases, you might try to develop your game to match your serve. If, for example, you have a powerful, flat first service, then you should by all means attempt to develop your net game, since the big serve and the net game go hand in hand. If, for some reason, you can't develop consistency at the net or if you simply prefer to play from the baseline, then forgo the big first serve. There's no point in wasting your strength if you're going to stay back. Go for the big serve occasionally to break up the rhythm, and serve a kicker or spinner the rest of the time.

One final warning about the serve: Don't try to overpower the ball when you're first learning or during the early part of any given season. The muscles used in the serve—especially the back muscles—are muscles that don't normally undergo such strain. It's a good idea to do a little exercising before trying to serve. You might try touching your toes, doing a few sit-ups, anything to get your back muscles in shape. You don't have to be particularly strong to play tennis, just so long as your muscles are well and evenly toned. If you have one muscle that is much weaker than the other, that's the one that's going to cause you difficulty. In most people, that trouble will occur in the back.

Start out slowly and condition these muscles bit by bit. Wait till you're fit before going all out. If you try to pulverize the ball the first day, you're likely to wind up with an injury.

The return of service you use depends largely on what kind of player you're faced with. If you're faced with a net rusher, you're going to be trying to chip short and get a lot of angles. You should be trying to put the ball on your opponent's toes, trying to make her bend and stretch as much as possible. When you're playing a baseline player, you should try to hit the ball back as deeply as possible,

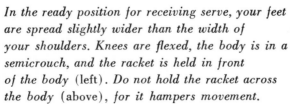

*In the ready position for receiving serve, your feet
are spread slightly wider than the width of
your shoulders. Knees are flexed, the body is in a
semicrouch, and the racket is held in front
of the body* (left). *Do not hold the racket across
the body* (above), *for it hampers movement.*

preferably to a corner, so that perhaps you yourself can come in to the net.

The ready position for receiving serve should be reasonably comfortable. Your feet should be slightly wider than the width of your shoulders, and your weight should be evenly distributed. The knees are flexed, and the body is in sort of a semicrouch position with the weight on the balls of the feet. Above all, you should be alert and ready to move in any direction. The racket is held out in front of the body, with the neck of the racket held in the nonracket hand. Do not hold the racket across your body but well out in front with your arms slightly bent, ready to turn quickly for either the backhand or forehand. Holding the racket neck with the nonracket hand makes it easy to change grips for forehand or backhand if you wish to. Some players prefer not to switch and will hit both forehand and backhand return of service with the same grip. It's simply a matter of how you were taught and of personal preference. Many players do a sort of hop just as the server strikes the ball to

get their body in motion. This little starting jump can be helpful, but if you mistime it, if you start too late, you may find yourself up on your toes when you should already be moving in one direction or the other.

Your position on the court when receiving serve is basically the same in either service court. You should be near the sideline, to cover the wide-angle serve, yet close enough in to cover a center-line serve. The service down the center line to either court is easier to cover than the serve to the outside line as it relies on only speed to get past you. The serve to the outside line combines pace with angle and requires an extra step to get to.

The depth at which you stand depends mainly on how your opponent serves. If she hits a deep flat first serve, you should be a yard or so behind the baseline, depending on how hard she hits it. Since the second serve usually doesn't have the depth and power of the first serve, you can move a yard or so inside the baseline to receive it.

A receiver facing a net-rushing player is not going to be hitting the same kind of forehand and backhand drives as she would be against a player who stays back. In trying to pass a net rusher, you should be standing in a little bit closer, chipping down on the ball or topspinning, trying to get the ball down on the toes of the incoming player. To accomplish this, you must take a smaller backswing and a shorter stroke, and hit the ball more in front of your body than for a long drive.

*Generally, for a hard first serve you stand
about a yard back of the baseline and move inside
the baseline for the second serve (opposite).
When the server stays back (below left and right),
you can take a full swing, but when she rushes
net (bottom left and right), you must shorten your
swing in order to keep the ball low over the net.*

Against a net rusher, a shortened backswing is
necessary for both forehand and backhand.
You must keep the ball low and play
the angles, easiest with a short backswing.

If your opponent is serving to the center line and coming to net in the middle of the court, you have the choice of three low returns to make—a chip to either side of her or straight at her. As long as these shots are low, they are all effective in making the net player bend and stretch on that first volley.

If your opponent is serving wide, however, you will be moved out of court and she will probably take up a net position more toward the side to which she has served. You are left with a difficult cross-court shot to make, since the angle will be acute, but an easy down-the-line shot.

If your opponent is serving and getting right up to the net very quickly, the lob is a good shot. It is difficult to lob on a return of serve, but if it comes off a few times, it will stop your opponent from charging quite so close to the net for her first volley. The lob in this case is shorter than the usual lob since it's hit from inside the baseline and is an aggressive shot. If you have confidence in your lob, you might try to hit a sharper angle than you normally would, since you've been given a good angle by the serve, assuming that it was a wide one. Even if the lob on your return of service doesn't win the point, it will serve the purpose of keeping your opponent from crowding the net quite so closely on the following points, and it might break her rhythm.

When playing against a player who stays at the baseline, you have more time for your

return. Since you need not crowd the return so much, you can take a full stroke. You also have more time to decide exactly where you want to hit the ball.

When you are playing against an opponent who invariably stays at the baseline, a good return of service is the dropshot. Even if it is not an outright winner, you may force your unwilling opponent to come to the net; if she is basically a baseline player, it will put pressure on her to be in foreign territory at the net, and she will be susceptible to being passed or beaten with an aggressive lob. The dropshot on return of service is a difficult shot,

ting cross-court forehands, trying to make them as short as possible in order to force the incoming server to hit up and give you or your partner an easy volley. If you're receiving on the backhand court, you'll be doing essentially the same thing—trying to chip short cross-courts to force the incoming player to hit up on the ball.

In doubles, the lob can be used especially well on return of service. If you lob over the person who's playing at net, you accomplish one of two things: Either you force the net player to move back or you force the incoming server to move over behind her partner. In either case, you've broken up their combination and given your side a lot of openings either to move in and volley the return away or, if they lob, to smash it away.

Learning to receive serve will undoubtedly come a lot easier than learning to serve. Remember that the service is probably the most unnatural of all strokes, especially for women. To repeat, I do recommend practicing without a ball or, for that matter, without a racket. It's terribly important to learn the right motion and practicing without racket and/or ball is perhaps the easiest way.

Learning to serve well is not easy, but you must do it in order to play decent tennis. You may play a passable, even excellent, game of tennis with only an adequate net game, but you'll never be able to play a competitive game without a good serve.

and there aren't really many players who can do it consistently. It's a valuable shot only when the percentage of errors you're forcing from it is high. If you're getting only one in three, it's not worth it. In this case, you're better off to get the ball deep to the baseline and try to work up the point from there.

In doubles, receiving strategy is much different. Although you're still going to be trying to chip or topspin the ball onto the incoming net player's toes, you've already got one opponent at the net, so you've got only half the court to work with. If you're receiving on the forehand side, you're going to be hit-

The Overhead
by Karen Krantzcke

The object in tennis is to force your opponent to give you a setup, and a setup often means an overhead.

Born in Brisbane, reared in Sydney, Australia, Karen Krantzcke was, at 6 feet 1½ inches, both the tallest woman on the Virginia Slims Tour and one of the prettiest. She was, until her untimely death, proof positive that a woman doesn't have to be tiny to be feminine.

After winning the Australian Junior Championship, Karen was a member of the official Australian team for two years. She began play on the international circuit in 1965, joining the Virginia Slims Tour in 1970.

Karen's best year was 1970. During that year she won the Federation Cup with Judy Dalton, she reached the quarterfinals in Wimbledon and South Africa, and she reached the semifinals in the Australian and French championships.

In 1971, Karen was ranked eighth in the world. Early that year, however, she developed hypoglycemia, a blood ailment, and missed nearly a year of play. Even after the long layoff and even though she was forced to miss several tournaments because of a minor injury, Karen managed to earn well in excess of $20,000 in 1972.

Karen Krantzcke died of a heart attack in April 1977.

When you begin a rally on court, your basic aim is to play your opponent into a position where she's forced to put up the easy shot that you can then put away with your overhead, or smash. The overhead is used a bit more in men's tennis because of the type of game they play—serve and volley—than it is in women's tennis, where a larger number of points are decided from the baseline. This fact, however, doesn't diminish the importance of the overhead in the women's game. Once you have forced your opponent out of position, once you have forced her to put up the easy lob, you must have the confidence and ability to put the shot away and not make a mistake of it. It's really quite heartbreaking to maneuver your opponent into a winning position—winning for you, that is—and then lose the point simply because you fail on your overhead.

Without getting into a lot of technicalities, let's talk about the grip for a moment. For the regular forehand stroke, you use essentially the "shake-hands" grip. For the backhand, most players move their hand a quarter-turn to the left, assuming they are right-handed. I smash with the backhand grip, and I think that most of the top professional girls do as well. It's a bit harder at first to smash with the backhand grip, but there are a lot of advantages to it once you've mastered it.

For instance, you'll find with the backhand grip that it's easier to come up over the ball, that it's easier to generate power, and that it's easier to control the ball. But as I've said, it's difficult to smash with the backhand grip when you've first started, so I don't advocate that the beginner go right out and try it. I think the beginner is better off to start with the forehand grip and gradually move around to the backhand grip. Don't move right around to the backhand grip straightaway, but take it in turns. Move your hand to the left just a slight bit; when you feel you've mastered that position, go a bit further, until finally you've moved all the way around.

One of the most important parts of the overhead is maneuverability. The moment you see your opponent lobbing to you, you've got to get back into position. When you hit the ball, it should be in front of your left foot—again assuming you are right-handed. If you were to let the ball hit the ground, your position should be such that the ball would strike several inches in front of your left foot. Therefore, you've got to get back quickly so that you can come forward into the ball as you hit it. This is not only one of the most important aspects of the overhead, it's also one of the most difficult.

A lot of players will leave the ground as they hit the overhead. Because I am tall, I myself seldom need to. I feel that you're more on balance if both feet are on the ground. Also, if your feet are on the ground, you can come forward as you hit the ball—and this is where you get a lot of your pace. There are times, of course, when you're at the net and your opponent lobs and you just don't have

Although a lot of players leave the ground when they hit an overhead, I feel you're better balanced if you keep both feet on the ground (left top and bottom). *Though the overhead is often confusing because the ball drops quickly at you, the motion is the same as for the serve* (below).

time to get back. In this case, you may have to leap off the ground to reach the ball. In most instances, however, you should be quick enough to get back so that you won't have to leave the ground.

    The overhead is essentially the same

*I strongly recommend that when learning the overhead,
you start the stroke with the racket
already cocked behind your head* (top left and right).
*Another good idea is to get your
nonracket hand over your head, pointing at the ball*
(bottom left and right). *It helps your balance.*

thing as the serve, the difference being that someone else has thrown the ball up for you. In the serve, you have a windup to get the motion going. When hitting the overhead, you have to dispense with this windup. The racket should be brought into place behind your head at almost the exact moment you begin to backpedal into position.

This might be a difficult concept to grasp, for if you watch the majority of the professionals, you'll see that most of them make one smooth stroke of the overhead. While they may not take as much of a windup as they would when serving, they don't set up with the racket cocked in back of them. They can afford to do this because they have been playing tennis for so long that their timing is grooved. But this is not the way I recommend to learn the stroke. Timing is much easier when your racket is already in position to hit. Remember, in tennis it's always very important to be ahead of the play rather than behind it. Be early, not late. With your racket back, you'll be much more sure to take advantage of whatever height you have.

As you get into position to hit the overhead, there are several important things to keep in mind. First of all, as I've already said, you should be back far enough so that the ball is coming down in front of your left foot. As you're backpedaling, your left, or nonracket, hand should be raised above your head, pointing at the ball. Raising your hand in this manner helps you to keep your balance and

serves another important purpose—it helps you to keep your eyes on the ball. Your eyes should be on the ball from the moment you start to backpedal until the moment you hit the ball. At the moment of contact your head should be tilted back. You are watching the ball. *Your head should remain in this position until the ball has left the strings.* Many players will drop their heads just before or just as they hit the ball. This causes mistakes.

When you've reached the correct position on court, stop by planting your back, or right, foot. As you begin the swing, your weight should begin to shift to your left, or forward, foot. As you hit the ball, your weight should be fairly evenly distributed between your feet, but it should be coming forward.

Your racket arm should be fully extended when you make contact with the ball. On the overhead, power comes from the shoulder; the minute you bend your elbow, you lose power and your overhead will tend to float.

After you make contact with the ball, swing right through. The overhead, once again, is just like the serve. Just as you swing right through on the serve, you should swing right through on the overhead. And, again, if you can manage to be moving forward when you hit the ball, you'll gain a lot of pace.

As I've already indicated, there are several different kinds of overheads. The first, basic, type of overhead is the flat one, the one that has no spin at all. You've maneuvered your opponent out of court, and you're trying

*As you set up,
weight is on the
back foot, but it
transfers to front
foot as you hit.
You move forward,
and your follow-
through is complete.*

to put the ball away. To hit the flat overhead, your racket simply comes straight through the ball. At the moment of impact the racket face is flat onto the ball, and you're reaching your full height up to the ball. Now, let's say you've hit a couple of flat overheads and your opponent has managed to return them. You might try to vary your attack a bit by using the slice overhead.

To hit the slice overhead, you must hit the ball when it's a little bit more off to your right. The racket face comes around the outside of the ball rather than straight through it. This imparts spin to the ball and causes it to "go off" as your opponent tries to return it. You should almost always hit the slice overhead to the forehand court so that the ball bounces away from your opponent.

The topspin overhead is usually used when you've been caught—that is, you haven't had time to get back into the correct position to hit the overhead. Since the ball is behind you, you naturally have to come back up over the top of the ball with the racket. As the racket comes up and over the ball, it imparts to the ball a forward rotation, which lends a bit of aggressiveness to a shot that might otherwise be on the weak side. Always try to place this particular shot as deep into court as you possibly can.

Generally, you should be trying for the flat smash. If you can't put the ball away, then try to vary your attack by using the slice smash. Reserve use of the topspin smash for

*To hit the slice overhead, you must hit
the ball when it's a little bit farther to your
right (middle). The racket face comes
around the oustide of the ball, causing spin.*

those times when the ball is behind you and there's nothing you can do about it. The type of smash you hit is mainly dependent on the position of your body in relation to the ball.

What you do after you've hit the overhead depends on your position on court and on how well you've hit the shot. As I said at the start, you essentially play the point to set up the overhead—the overhead should be the winning shot. If you are fairly close to the net and you feel you've hit a good overhead, you should immediately follow your shot to the net. Hopefully your opponent won't even be able to get her racket on the ball, but if she does, the chances are that it will be an easy matter for you to finish off the point with, for example, a short volley.

If, however, your opponent is lobbing really well and she's got you all the way back on the baseline, then obviously you can't run all the way in to the net. In this case, you should return to the center of the court, near the baseline, and wait to see what develops.

Normally, as I've said, if you simply hit away at the overhead, it wins—assuming, of course, that you manage to keep it in court. In spite of this, I feel that you should almost always aim your smash to your opponent's backhand. The reasoning behind this goes as follows: Almost every time you hit an overhead, it will be because your opponent has lobbed, and most players will try to hit their lob to your backhand side. You therefore have to move around the lob so that you can take it on

Sometimes before you hit the overhead, it will be necessary to let the ball bounce. When it does, the stroke remains the same in all aspects. Don't forget the importance of moving forward.

your overhead rather than with your backhand smash. Most people don't have the power—or the confidence—on their backhand smash that they have on their forehand. In doing this, in moving around the lob to get in on your forehand side, you've positioned yourself far over to your backhand side. It's therefore much safer to smash the ball cross-court to your opponent's backhand. If you smash it down the line and don't put it away and if your opponent manages to get to the ball, she'll simply hit a cross-court forehand. You'll find it very difficult to get to the ball because the ball will be moving away from you at a sharp angle into a wide-open court.

Aside from the fact that hitting your overhead to the forehand side opens up the

When handling a tough lob, one that you're not sure you can put away, you should try to hit the ball to your opponent's backhand corner, where she should have trouble.

court and therefore isn't sound strategically, there is another reason to hit to the backhand —it's simply more difficult for your opponent to handle this shot. I'd say that perhaps 80 percent of your smashes should be aimed at your opponent's backhand. The only time you should smash down the line is when you are completely confident that you can put the ball away with ease.

On some lobs—lobs that are particularly good or especially high—it's best to let the ball bounce before hitting it. In most cases these lobs will be landing a yard or so from the baseline. The same rules apply to hitting an overhead after the ball has bounced as do to hitting it while the ball is still in the air. In this situation, however, you can't really try for the put-away. This is one of the times when it's best to use the slice smash. Since hitting the overhead after the ball has bounced is a difficult shot, you'll see a lot of players who will let the ball drop past its peak and then take it with a regular forehand or backhand. The really good players, however, will try to utilize the height of the bounce by bringing their rackets over or around the ball. While it's best not to try for the winner here, there's no reason not to take the most aggressive shot possible.

For myself, of course, because of my height, it's very seldom that I get a bounce that's high enough for me to smash. So what you do with the lob that has bounced will depend a lot on your height. For some of the

*Here I've had to let the ball bounce. I haven't
had time to get behind the ball and to come forward.
I can't take an aggressive shot, so I've hit
a slice overhead in the same way I'd hit the serve.*

smaller girls—Billie Jean King and Rose-mary Casals, for instance—the bounce is very often just the right height for the overhead.

In conjunction with this topic, there's another point I should mention. You'll remember that I said that the overhead should always be hit with a straight arm, at the full extension of your height. Sometimes the ball will come to you at a level—whether or not you've allowed the ball to bounce—that's not quite high enough for you to smash at your full height. In this situation you should bend your knees and get down so that your arm is still fully extended when you hit the ball. You might call this a sort of semioverhead. The main thing is to bend your knees instead of your arm and to still follow through.

Your height probably affects the way you hit the overhead more than it does any other stroke, with the exception of the serve. Normally, the smaller girl moves better than the taller one and can get back into position much more quickly. On the court, physical attributes have a way of balancing out—there are advantages and disadvantages to being tall, just as there are advantages and disadvantages to being short.

One of the most common mistakes made by tennis players is trying for extra power on the overhead. Power in the overhead comes basically from two places—your shoulder and your rhythm, or timing. If your stroke is smooth and fluid and if you hit the ball at your full height, the power will come natu-

In summary: Get the racket into position behind your head, point your finger at the ball, transfer your weight, and move forward when you hit.

rally. If you grit your teeth and start trying to kill the ball, all that will happen is you'll start missing shots.

I think that for the beginning player the groundstrokes—the forehand and the backhand—are the first strokes to be learned. After that come the serve and then the volley. After some degree of competence has been reached in these areas, then I think you can move to the overhead. It's particularly important that a beginner have the mechanics of the serve working before she tries the overhead. The overhead is one of the more difficult shots in tennis, and there's no point in trying to teach it to a beginner until she has begun to develop a sense of rhythm.

There is really only one way to learn the overhead, and that's to go out on the court and get someone to send up lob after lob to you. The overhead is an especially tiring shot, so I recommend relatively short practice sessions, particularly at first. While you're practicing the overhead, concentrate on footwork and mobility. In any shot in tennis, footwork is extremely important. In the overhead, footwork and timing are the two most important factors. I myself find that when I get caught on the overhead, the reason is that I just haven't gotten back far enough and I'm being forced to hit the ball while it's back behind my head. It's a good idea, therefore, to overcompensate for this tendency when you're practicing. What I mean by this is that you should move back farther than you need to and then move

back forward into the ball. After you've developed your timing and learned to judge the ball correctly, you can then move back only as far as you need to and still be certain that the ball is in front of you. But remember, no matter how proficient you become at hitting the overhead, you are still liable to make errors in judgment—so that it's always better to move back farther than you need to than to get caught short.

Once you have developed a sound overhead, you'll find that your chances of winning matches have greatly increased. Having a strong, consistent overhead takes a lot of pressure off you and puts it on your opponent. When you're rallying, your opponent knows that she can't afford to send up a weak shot because you'll simply put it away. The added

pressure will often cause her to do just that.

Having a good overhead makes your net game immeasurably stronger. If your opponent has respect for your overhead, then you have effectively taken away one of her shots—the lob. She knows that when you're at net, she can't afford to hit a weak lob, so she's more likely to go for the passing shots—which are likely to be wild, since she's probably not in position to hit them properly. But she knows that if she does give you the overhead, you're probably going to win the point anyway, so she may as well try for the other shot. If, on the other hand, you haven't developed your overhead and your opponent knows that it's a weak spot, you'll have a very difficult time trying to play at net.

To summarize the basic points of the overhead: As you go back for the overhead, your racket should immediately go into position behind your head. Your head should be up and your eyes should be on the ball. Your left hand should be in the air, pointing at the ball. When you've reached the correct position on court—the one where the ball is in a trajectory that will cause it to land several inches in front of your left foot—you stop by planting your back foot, which for a right-hander is the right foot. Then, as you swing through the ball—with your arm extended to its full reach for maximum power—your weight shifts from the back foot to the forward foot, so that at the moment of impact, your weight is coming forward. You should be side on to the net, your head should still be up, and you should follow through.

The Volley

by Rosemary Casals

To say that the volley is an integral
part of the net game is to miss the point.
The volley *is* the net game.

At 5 feet 2½ inches, Rosemary Casals is one of the shortest tennis players on the circuit, but what she lacks in size she makes up in speed, agility, and all-around talent. Born in San Francisco in 1948, Rosie learned to play tennis in Golden Gate Park. "My father used to play doubles every Saturday morning. I'd hang around and beg to play. His friends would take turns giving me a quarter to go ride the merry-go-round, but when they ran out of change, they'd have to give up and let me play."

Unlike most players, Rosie can't remember a time when she couldn't hit the ball. She won the first tournament she ever entered, for nine-year-olds and under, defeating the top-seeded player in the first round. Since then she has won numerous national titles and has twice been ranked as high as the number-four woman tennis player in the world. Nine times she has held the number-one ranking in doubles, eight with Billie Jean King, and, in 1977, with Chris Evert.

An aggressive, attacking player, "Rosebud" was a finalist in the U.S. Open in both 1970 and 1971 and was a semifinalist at Wimbledon for three years in a row. With Billie Jean King, she won the doubles title at Wimbledon in 1967, 1968, 1970, 1971, and 1973. In 1977, she finished fourth in the Virginia Slims Championships; in 1979, she was twice a singles semifinalist, and in doubles made the semifinals or better in six Avon Championship events. Rosie has played World Team Tennis since 1974.

*To learn to hit the ball out front, it's
often a good idea to try catching, or stopping, the
ball with your bare hand first. Once you get
the feel, try it with a racket (opposite),
but hold it at the throat first to better
understand that the racket is an extension
of your hand.*

The volley is a shot, on either the forehand or backhand side, that is hit before the ball has struck the ground on your side of the court. Volleys are hit while the ball is still in the air and usually before the ball has passed over the service line.

To say that the volley is an integral part of the net game would be to miss the point. The volley *is* the net game. I am not saying, however, that to play good tennis, you have to have a superior net game. There are many women playing at a competitive level who prefer to play from the backcourt. You do not have to play net to be either aggressive or offensive. Nancy Richey is a perfect example. She is a superb groundstroker with a competent volley. Whether or not you want to refine your volley depends on what style of game you want to play.

Of course, I recommend you learn how to volley and how to volley well. The more well-rounded your game is, the better tennis player you will be. Sometimes a net game is vital to beating a certain opponent. And finally, look at the records. The two dominant women on the tour today are Billie Jean King and Margaret Court. Good net games? The best.

The main thing to think about at first is to hit the ball out in front. To develop a feel for the volley, generally a beginner will start by simply catching the ball. As I toss the ball to her, I'll have her catch—or even just stop—the ball out in front of her body. After she's become proficient at stopping or catching the ball with her bare hand, then she can begin to practice with a racket. This transition can be made quite smoothly if the beginner keeps in mind that the racket is merely an extension of the hand.

Your next concern with the volley is that it should always be hit out toward the baseline. A lot of beginners assume that the volley should be hit down—it shouldn't. A good volley should be hit out in front and pushed out to an area within a foot of the baseline.

After you've got these two concepts firmly in mind, your concern should be footwork. Footwork is very important in the volley. It's important to get to the ball in time to position yourself to make the shot. A lot of players will just extend themselves or their rackets, forgetting about footwork. This causes them to hit weak, defensive shots rather than aggressive, offensive shots, as well as putting them off balance or out of position.

If you're going to your right to make a forehand volley, assuming that you're right-handed, your left foot should be out in front. Conversely, on the backhand volley, your right foot should be out in front.

Naturally, a lot of times we're put in a situation where it's desperation that rules—we have to get to the ball and we'll get there any way we can and hit it any way we can. But the basic technique is still there—getting the racket into proper position and hitting the ball out in front. Generally the footwork will follow after that and be at least adequate. But for the beginner, it's a good idea to concentrate on footwork. As you move to the right to make the forehand volley, be sure that your left foot is out in front and that your left shoulder is turned toward the net. The same thing applies in reverse on the backhand side —make sure your right foot is in front and your right shoulder is turned toward the net.

Don't change the position of the racket during the volley. The racket head should stay out in front and should remain more or less perpendicular to the ground. The racket head should never be twisted prior to contact with the ball.

Never swing on a volley. The volley should be a blocking action. Block with the racket just as you blocked with your hand in the beginning exercise. Remember that the racket is just an extension of your hand. As you see the ball coming to either side, you simply thrust the racket forward to make con-

On the forehand volley (opposite), *your weight and your left foot are forward. On the backhand volley, weight and right foot are forward and the shoulder is turned toward the net* (below).

tact. Eventually you'll develop the feel and begin to guide the ball. Later on—hopefully —you'll actually place the ball.

Basically I use the Eastern grip, which is the grip used by most of the players. The Eastern is the "shake hands" grip. Some players use the Continental grip, which is a modified version of the Eastern. For the Continental, you turn your hand a quarter of a turn counterclockwise, or to the left. Many players have a tendency to place the thumb of their racket hand on the back of the grip when hitting the backhand. Personally, I wouldn't advise this. The thumb in this position does compensate for weakness early on, but eventually, as you play, you'll build up the necessary strength. Once you have developed these muscles, the thumb movement is an unnecessary one and will only get in your way.

There is also the Western grip, which nowadays is virtually nonexistent, at least in top-level tennis. It was used extensively maybe 50 or 60 years ago, but today there are no good volleyers who use the Western. Just for historical interest, to get the Western grip you lay the racket flat on the ground and then pick it up as though it were a frying pan.

There are many modified versions of these grips. For instance, some of the girls will spread their fingers evenly along the grip. This really isn't necessary, it's just a matter of personal preference. There are other variations that certain players will use. For instance, sometimes a player who uses a Conti-

nental will slip into an Eastern if the volley is a very high volley and she wants to get on top of the ball and have a little more power. Many players feel they can achieve a bit of added power by changing grips on certain shots. But, again, it really isn't necessary to do this, and the beginner should not worry about it.

Once more, the volley is basically a block. You don't want to get into a situation where you're swinging freely as though the shot were a groundstroke. You want to use as little swing as possible. When you're up at net, the ball is covering a shorter distance and is coming at you very fast. You're trying to cut sharp angles, so you simply don't have time to take any kind of a swing. If you do try to swing, you're going to miss a lot of shots.

When hitting the volley, you should try to utilize the speed your opponent has placed on the ball. It's not necessary to hit an extremely crisp volley. The more important thing is placement. If you're standing at the net and your opponent hits the ball right to you, all you have to do is direct the ball to an open spot. It's really a very simple shot when the ball comes right to you. If there's a lot of pace and you have to move a great deal, then it's a little bit harder to coordinate all the movements—but it's still not necessary to hit the volley hard.

If you should happen to watch a professional tournament, you may begin to feel that everything I'm saying doesn't hold true. Everyone, of course, has her own style of

Although the volley is basically a blocking action with little, if any, follow-through (left), I have a tendency to follow through more than most (right). I don't recommend the follow-through for beginning players.

play, and not everybody's volley is going to be the same. Almost every girl on the pro tour has a slightly different way of hitting the volley. Whatever the style, for the most part, the volleys are more than adequate and get the job done. I myself have a tendency to take a bit of a swing and to follow through a bit. Some other players do the same thing. But we're talking here about players who have been at the game for 15 or 20 years and have established their own styles.

When you hit a volley, I would say that generally your arm should be well extended in front of you and your wrist should be locked. This rule, however, is a difficult one to insist on. Obviously you're not going to extend your arm if the ball is going to hit you in the stomach. As in all tennis shots, you have to be flexible. When you're at net, you've got about half the time to prepare that you have at the baseline. The shots are coming at you very quickly, and you have to more or less take them as you find them. If you've got the time, then, of course, you should prepare, but you can't have perfect form on every shot. And, as I've said, almost every player hits the volley a little bit differently. Some hit with a straight arm, some with a bent arm, some with an elbow extended. The important thing is to hit out in front and to do something aggressive with your volley.

A lot of people say that on the volley, the racket head should never drop below the level of your wrist. I don't think this is necessarily

My arm is comfortably extended, I'm hitting the ball out front, and my wrist is tightly locked. Although the ball is in a bad (high) position, you can see that I'm still being aggressive.

true. There are times when you have to drop the racket head—on a low volley, for instance. The low volley is probably the toughest volley to hit. The volleys at waist or shoulder height are relatively easy, but when a volley is down around your ankles, it can really give you trouble. It's important, however, that you be able to hit the low volley, since that's the kind a good opponent is going to try to give you.

On the low volley, bend your knees. You've got to get right down to the ball so that your eyes are almost on a level with the racket and the ball. A lot of players will get lazy and just sort of stick their racket down to the ball. This is a kind of desperation shot, since the player who does it is simply trying to get the ball back over the net rather than trying to do something with it. I've said that it's all right for your racket head to occasionally drop below the level of your wrist on the volley, but I don't mean by this that it's all right to just reach down for the ball. If you want to do anything with your shot—and you always should —then you have to be mobile and get down to the ball.

For the most part, and especially at the beginning, you should consider the volley to be a flat shot—that is, you shouldn't try to impart spin to the ball. As you advance, however, as you gain confidence and proficiency with the volley, there will be some things you can do with spin. There is, for instance, the stop, or drop, volley. In the stop volley, you

*The stop volley is hit with the racket under
the ball and the face slightly open. If done well,
the stop volley will actually bounce backward.
It's a shot that takes many years to develop.*

take a ball that is coming at you at a fairly
rapid pace and give it a slight undercut—that
is, you hit under the ball with the racket face
slightly opened—so that the ball just barely
clears the net and has backspin on it. If done
well, the stop volley will actually bounce
backward into the net so that your opponent
has almost zero chance of getting to it. The
stop volley requires a great deal of touch—in
fact, it's also called the touch volley. The
reason for this is that not only do you hit the
ball with backspin, but you also have to sort
of pull back on the racket at the moment of
impact. The touch volley is a very difficult
shot, and very few players can do it well. It
takes many, many years and a lot of experience to develop the feel for it—many players
never do.

It is possible to top a volley—to hit it
with topspin—but I wouldn't recommend this
shot. I must admit that I do it fairly often and
that there are some other players as well who
will take a fairly high volley, say shoulder
height, and topspin it for a winner. But again,
this is not a percentage shot. It takes a lot of
experience and a lot of concentration to do it.
As I've already indicated, on some occasions
you'll find a lot of players doing things that
aren't in the book.

Generally a put-away volley will be
cross-court. When you're coming to net after
serving, for instance, and the ball comes to
you on the forehand side, your put-away shot
will be cross-court. A setup shot, a shot to put

you into position to make a winning shot, would probably be down the line to your opponent's backhand as you move to net to force her to try either to put the ball past you or, hopefully, to hit it directly to you. Naturally, in this case, wherever your opponent is not is where you're going to hit your volley. If you're playing on a fast surface, the best shot in this case is usually a short volley, one that strikes the court inside the service line.

On the backhand side, the same general rules apply. When you go cross-court with the volley, you're going for the winner. When you go down the line, you're going for the approach shot, the setup shot, to get you into position to win the point on the next shot. Don't misunderstand. From either side a shot hit down the line can be played as a winner if your opponent is in another area of the court.

Remember that when you miscue on a winning shot—or a shot that was intended to be a winner—then you're very likely to be passed. For this reason it's very important to put the ball where your opponent is not or at least in a position where you can't be hurt.

When you want to go cross-court with the volley, you have to hit the ball way out in front. If you meet the ball way out in front, your body and your swing will automatically direct the ball cross-court. By the same token, if you want to send the ball down the line, you should simply hit it late. Some pro players will, at times, redirect the ball by changing the position of the racket or the wrist. But

again, this maneuver is not for the beginner; it's for someone who has been playing the game for years and has developed the capability to be aware of exactly where the racket head is at all times.

I've said that your wrist should basically be locked when you hit the volley. On occasions, you'll find that it's slightly tilted backward or forward, depending on your position and on what you are trying to do with the ball. If, for instance, you want to hit a very sharp cross-court angle from your forehand side to your opponent's forehand side, then the position of your wrist will be such that the racket is almost facing you, since you'll be, in effect, hitting the ball sideways.

As much as is possible, I feel that all strokes in tennis should be taught at the same time. First, of course, a beginner should learn the basics of hitting groundstrokes from both sides. A lot of beginners will tend to shy away from hitting backhands, although the backhand is actually one of the easier shots in the game—you're hitting through the ball, you don't have to hit across your body, so it's actually a more natural stroke than is the forehand. You can have a very easy, simple, basic backhand and still be efficient with it. With the forehand, you'll get involved with a lot more problems, such as hitting across the ball, hitting under it, hitting over it, and slicing.

After the beginner has learned the fundamentals of groundstrokes—say after the third or fourth lesson—then she should go up

*When you come to the net,
you cut the angles and force your opponent
to be more accurate.*

to the net and begin to work on the volley. At the same time, she should begin to learn a little about all the strokes—the serve, the lob, the smash, the dropshot.

The best—perhaps the only—way to practice the volley is to get a partner to practice with. You should both stand in at the net position and simply feed each other volleys.

All the while you should be thinking about hitting the ball out in front, not actually swinging, but just blocking the ball back over the net. Once you and your practice partner have developed a bit of consistency, you can have a pretty nice little game at the net.

As I've said, the volley is an offensive shot. When you're at the net, you should be attacking at all times—and I personally feel that a player should get to the net every chance she has. When you're at net, you've cut off your opponent's angles and given her a lesser amount of room to hit the ball past you. When you're at the baseline, your opponent has a lot more room—she can hit the ball almost anywhere she wants to. As you shorten the distance, you cut off the angles and force your opponent to be more accurate.

Many beginners are reluctant to go to the net—maybe I should say that they're afraid to go to the net. This is simply because they haven't yet learned how to be combative—and the idea of a ball coming at you at 100 miles an hour can be a little unsettling at first. With practice, you'll learn that all you have to do is stick your racket out and you're not going to

get hurt. In fact, even if the ball should hit you, you're not going to get hurt—it might sting a little, but a tennis ball is, after all, pretty soft. Eventually you'll be able to determine the speed of the ball in relation to your body and racket and be able to coordinate all your movements with accurate results.

There are still two types of volleys I haven't talked about. One is the half volley. The half volley is hit after the ball has struck the ground and has begun its upward ascent. Generally, the ball is hit immediately after it bounces—in the shortest time possible after it strikes the ground. Although the half volley can be hit from anywhere in the court, it is usually hit from the midcourt. It is not a planned shot, but more of a retrieve when you've been caught—and midcourt is where you're likely to be caught. A good way to describe the half volley is to liken it to a drop kick in soccer. The shot should be hit with a half stroke and, if you're advanced enough, with the racket coming over the ball. Remember, you've got to be aggressive on volleys.

The other volley is the lob volley, which is used by higher-level players and is used more in doubles than in singles, when all four players are at net. It's usually an offensive shot which offers the element of surprise. The lob volley is just what it sounds—a lob off the volley. It is never hit with topspin.

The volley takes practice—all shots in tennis do. You have to be able to follow the ball, to know where it's going and what to do

with it. Practice will enable you to do this—practice and good reflexes. Naturally, you can't learn to have quick reflexes—you either have them or you don't. But almost everyone is quick enough to become at least adequate with the volley. And an adequate net game is surely a hundred times better than no net game at all.

The type of court you're playing on will affect the type of game you play. On clay, for instance, there's less need for a volleying game. In fact, a lot of players who learn the game on clay never develop a net game. My advice is to learn to play on all types of surface. Don't develop a one-dimensional game that you're stuck with no matter what type of court you're on or what kind of opponent you're facing. To really enjoy the game, to really play it well, you must be flexible. It will take longer to develop a sound, all-around game, but in the long run it will be much more satisfying and rewarding.

131

The Lob and the Dropshot

by Kerry Reid

The lob is one of the most effective weapons in tennis, and the dropshot should be attempted at least once a game.

Born in 1947 in Mosman, Australia, Kerry Melville Reid called Melbourne her hometown from the time she was five years old. Since her marriage to touring pro Raz Reid, however, she makes her home in Greenville, South Carolina.

Both Kerry's parents were good tennis players, and it was through them that she was introduced to the game. After winning the Australian Junior Championship, she joined the official Australian team in 1966 and made her first appearance on the international circuit that year. She immediately established herself as a power to be reckoned with by upsetting Billie Jean King in the second round at the U.S. Open. Eleven times ranked in the world's top 10 since 1966, Kerry held down fifth position from 1972 to 1974. During her career, she has earned 24 international titles and more than $600,000, with 1978 being her most financially rewarding year to date ($160,000).

In singles, Kerry has been in the finals or semifinals of virtually every major tournament in the world. With fellow Australian Karen Krantzcke, she twice won the U.S. Clay Court doubles. With Wendy Turnbull, she won the Wimbledon and U.S. indoor doubles and was a finalist in the U.S. Open, all in 1978.

At 5 feet 5½ inches, 125 pounds, Kerry is shy and smiling off court but determined and aggressive on court. Her game is one of precision and accuracy.

The lob is a shot that is beginning to come back into tennis. Three or four years ago, professional tennis players—both men and women—seldom used the lob. Nowadays, if you watch the top professionals, you'll see that they lob an extraordinary number of times during a match. Sometimes it seems as though almost every second shot is a lob. When you realize just how often they do use the lob, you'll have an idea of how important a shot it is. I've only just recently begun to see the light myself. At one time, I used to try to blast my groundshots past everyone. Needless to say, that didn't always work. Now I've learned that not only can I use the lob as a potent offensive and defensive weapon, but by so doing, I can increase the effectiveness of my passing shots.

In men's tennis, the lob you'll see most often is the offensive, topspin lob. Although some girls can hit the topspin lob and hit it quite well, the lob used most often in women's tennis is the defensive, underspin lob. There are at least a couple of reasons for this. One is strength. To hit a topspin lob takes a bit more strength in the wrist than most girls have, although, as I've said, there are a few girls who can do it with no difficulty. Another reason is speed. Since most men cover the court very quickly, the defensive lob is not always effective against them. In men's tennis, therefore, the topspin lob is almost a necessity. Women, on the other hand, tend to be slower in moving back. Because of this, the

undercut, defensive lob usually gets the job done quite well.

The lob can be used to good advantage in several situations and for several purposes. You can often use the lob simply for the element of surprise. When your opponent isn't expecting it, a lob can catch her off guard and throw off her rhythm. Another time that the lob is invaluable is when you've been forced right out of court. You're off balance and out of position, so you just throw up a high lob. An underspin, defensive lob takes a long time to get down to the other end of the court, and you can use this time to get yourself back into position. You've saved the point and recovered, and it's almost like starting the point over again.

The lob is especially useful when you're playing against a player who serves and volleys all the time. As I pointed out earlier, there's no way that you can keep blasting your groundstrokes past such a player. If a person is playing a serve and volley game, chances are that she's a good volleyer. And every time she picks off one of your passing shots, she's going to get more confident. If you can mix your passing shots with lobs, you'll put a bit of hesitation in your opponent's mind. Even if she manages to get to one or two of your lobs with her overhead, you're still serving the purpose of tiring her out. Also, once you've made her uncertain of whether you're going to hit a groundstroke or a lob, she's likely to start playing a bit farther

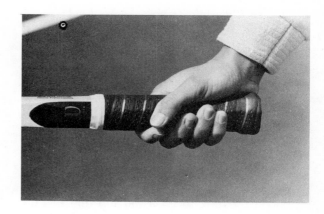

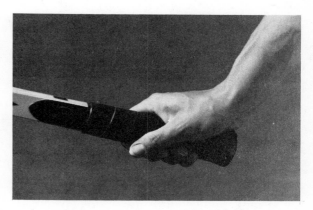

back from the net. This gives you both more time and a better angle for your groundshots.

The grip I use for the lob is the Continental grip—the same grip I use for the backhand, the serve, the volley, and the smash. To get this grip, you start with the "shake hands" grip—that is, you place the palm of your hand on the racket face and then slide your hand down the shaft to the handle. This is also called Eastern or forehand grip. To move into the Continental grip, a right-handed person should move her hand a quarter-turn counterclockwise, or to the left; a left-handed person should move it clockwise, or to the right.

Once you've got the correct grip, the next thing to think about is footwork. If at all possible, you should try to get your side to the net and play the lob the same way you would a normal forehand or backhand. A lot of times, of course, you're out of position, or you've had to run a long way to get to the ball and you don't have time to get into the proper position. In this case, you're better off to worry about getting the ball back rather than about how your form looks.

Remember to keep the racket head low. Drop the racket head below the level of your wrist, get the racket head right under the ball, and open the face of the racket. Having the racket face open as you strike the ball imparts underspin to the ball. The spin on the ball adds control and keeps the ball from flying out of the court. Topspin, which I'll talk a bit more about later on, also gives added control.

To get the Continental grip, start with the Eastern grip (top), *which I use for the forehand. Turn your hand a quarter-turn counterclockwise* (above), *and you'll be in the correct position.*

For the backspin lob, drop the racket head below the level of your wrist, get the racket head right under the ball, and open the face.

It is also possible to hit a flat lob that has no spin at all. You can do this by keeping the racket face parallel to the ground and hitting almost straight up. The flat lob, however, is seldom used, and I don't really recommend it.

When hitting the lob, keep your backswing to a minimum. All you need is a small, circular motion to get your racket moving. As in all shots in tennis, I believe that you should keep your eyes on the ball. I know it's a cliché, but it's amazing how many players, top professionals included, have difficulty because they don't watch the ball until after it has left the strings.

Don't be afraid to hit the lob. A short lob is ineffective—in fact, it will probably lose the point for you. Its better to lose the point by hitting the lob long than it is to hit the lob short and let your opponent blast you off the court with her overhead. Hitting the ball too lightly is a common error. And the reason that most people make the error of hitting the ball too lightly is that they are not following through. For some reason, many people seem to follow through only halfway on the lob. You follow through completely on your forehand, backhand, and serve, and you should do the same on the lob. It's very important to follow through high—right up to the sky. I'm talking here about the underspin lob. The follow-through on the topspin lob is different.

So far I haven't said much about how to actually hit the topspin lob. One reason for this is, as I've said, the topspin lob is a shot

*For the topspin lob, get sideways to the net,
drop the racket face low, and at impact, twist your
wrist and forearm over in a rolling motion.*

that is used much more often in men's tennis than it is in women's tennis—perhaps about 5 percent of all lobs hit in women's tennis are topspin. Another reason is that the topspin lob is a shot that should be used mainly by advanced players. Before you even begin to practice with the topspin lob, you should completely master the undercut lob. The topspin lob is a great shot when it comes off, but it's hardly what you'd call a high-percentage shot.

To hit the topspin lob, you begin the shot the same way you begin the underspin lob. You should move into position, get sideways to the net—if time allows—and drop the racket face low, below the level of your wrist. The racket face is once again open as you begin the stroke, but instead of hitting more or less straight up, you hit over, or up the back of the ball. At the moment of impact, you should twist your wrist and your forearm forward in a rolling motion. This motion imparts forward spin to the ball. The trajectory of the topspin lob is much lower than that of the undercut, and the ball moves with greater speed. When the ball strikes, assuming that your opponent hasn't managed to hit it with her overhead—and if she has, you can be sure that the topspin has caused her some trouble—it just sort of shoots off very quickly. It's an attacking shot.

With both lobs, the underspin and the overspin, the racket face should be facing the sky—or should be parallel to the ground, to put it another way—when you begin the stroke. On the underspin, the racket face

should be in approximately the same position when you finish the stroke as it was when you began. On the topspin, you're hitting up and over the ball, so the racket face should be, in fact, closed when you finish the stroke. On the underspin lob, the follow-through should be straight up toward the sky. The follow-through on the topspin lob, however, is more like the follow-through on a normal forehand or backhand—that is, across your body. The racket face winds up on the left side of your body, assuming that you are right-handed and have hit a forehand topspin lob, perhaps just slightly higher than it would have been had you hit a normal forehand.

The lob can be hit with either the forehand or the backhand with equal effectiveness. The general rules we've been covering apply to both wings.

The placement of the lob is of primary importance. As I pointed out earlier, the lob must be deep. If you hit a lob to the area of the service line, all you've done is given your opponent an easy setup for her overhead—which usually means that you've lost the point.

Now, assuming that you are always going to hit the lob deep, which part of the court do you want to aim for? Only occasionally—very occasionally—do you want to hit the lob down the line. The only reason to hit the lob down the line—except in doubles, which I'll talk about later—is to catch your opponent by sur-

In the follow-through for the topspin lob,
racket face ends up closed (below). In the
follow-through for the underspin lob (right), racket
face is open and points toward the sky.

prise. And, if you're going to catch her by surprise, then obviously you can't do it often.

Normally, the best place to hit the lob is on the diagonal—to either the forehand corner or the backhand corner. By hitting the lob on a diagonal, you accomplish a number of purposes. For one thing, the ball will be in the air for a longer time; this gives you more time to get into position, assuming that you've hit the lob because you were forced out of court. Hitting the lob on a diagonal also causes your opponent to cover a greater distance on the court. This means that when she gets to the ball, she'll be much less likely to hit a strong return. It also means that as the match wears on, she's going to tire.

Basically, then, you should aim your lobs for the deep corners. Of the two corners, I much prefer—and I think most other players do as well—the backhand corner. Hitting to the backhand corner forces your opponent to run back to the ball at an awkward angle. Once she gets to the ball, there's really very little she can do with it.

If you've hit a good lob, you should always follow it to the net. Of course, there are times when the reason you've hit the lob is that you were forced so far out of position that there was nothing else you could do. In this instance, you may not have time to get all the way to the net and you'll have to settle for getting back to center court near the baseline. Let's assume, however, that you've hit the lob because your opponent is playing serve and

volley. You hit the lob to her backhand corner and then take the net yourself. You will now be in a commanding position to cut off any return your opponent will try. It is likely that she will hit a weaker groundstroke than usual because she will be off balance from chasing the lob. It should therefore be an easy put-away volley for you. There is also a chance that your opponent will lob back after a shot like this. However, it should be an easy setup for your smash. As with any shot in tennis, occasionally your opponent can hit a brilliant shot that will win the point, but nine times out of ten, the net player will win the point with these tactics.

The wind, of course, affects lobs more than it does other shots. If you're playing in a crosswind, you will have to make adjustments. You may, for instance, have to hit your lobs just a bit lower than you normally do. If the wind is blowing from your left to your right and you want to hit to the backhand corner, you may have to aim more for the center of the court than normally and let the wind carry the ball to the corner. If the wind is from your right to your left, you may have to hit the ball actually outside the court and let the wind bring it back in. This is very tricky business, however, and if the wind is very strong or is gusting, the best idea is probably to keep your lobs to a minimum or to aim always for the center of the court.

When the wind is blowing lengthwise down the court and is at your back, don't try to lob. The lob is very hard to control in this situation, and even if you just tap it—unless you have a severe topspin—the ball is likely to sail not only out of the court but right over the fence. Wait until you've changed sides and the wind is in your face. Then you can hit the lob as hard as you like and the chances of its going out are very slim. The first time or two you hit the lob into the wind, the wind may hold it up and cause it to drop short. You don't have to worry too much about this because the wind is affecting the flight of the ball and your opponent therefore is going to have a more difficult time putting the ball away than she would on a normal lob that fell short.

The lob is used even more in doubles than it is in singles. You can use it very well on return of service. As the server comes in, you can lob over the person at net and then go to the net yourself. This puts your opponent off balance and gives your side the initiative, since you have control of the net. The lob can also be used in doubles when all four of you are at the net. In this situation, you can use a lob volley, which is a very difficult shot but at the same time very effective. The lob volley is basically the same as the lob, the only difference being that you don't allow the ball to bounce. Once again, it's a very difficult shot and one that I don't recommend to the beginner. But if all four players are at net or if your opponents are just sitting right on the net, try smashing a couple of volleys at their feet and then coming back with the lob volley.

If you can bring the shot off, chances are it will win the point for you.

If you're playing an opponent who is short in stature, you should increase the proportion of lobs you hit. The smaller girls usually move well, but the lob is still quite effective against them. It's much easier to lob over a short opponent than it is a tall one. If you're playing a tall opponent, your margin for error is cut down. By that I mean that if your lobs aren't hit almost perfectly, to just the right depth, you'll find that your opponent is picking them off with her overhead and turning them into winners. The smaller girl will almost invariably have to run all the way back to the baseline and play the weaker shot off the bounce.

Almost all the top girls on the pro tour have exceptionally good lobs, and I think this points up the fact that the lob is a key shot in tennis. In teaching a beginner to play tennis, I think I'd start with the groundstrokes and then the serve, but I'd teach her the lob before getting to the volley or the smash. I guess that's just another way of saying how I rank the importance of the different shots.

Remember, don't be afraid to hit the lob. The lob is a stroke just like all the others, and it should be hit with the same confidence and firmness. And follow through, don't just slap at the ball. If you follow through, with a smooth fluid movement, your lob will be high and deep—and that's exactly what you want.

Mix your passing shots with lobs and don't fall into a pattern. If you can keep your opponent guessing, if you can get her to the point where she's uncertain whether you are going to try a passing shot or a lob, then your lob is going to be effective.

The dropshot is a shot that is used mainly on slow surfaces, such as clay, rather than on faster surfaces, such as cement. In fact, on fast surfaces the dropshot shouldn't be used at all. You'll also find that the dropshot works better on cool, damp days than it does on hot, dry ones. And, like the lob, it is better hit into the wind than with it.

The grip for the forehand dropshot is the shake hands, or Eastern, grip. The grip for the backhand dropshot is the backhand, or Continental, grip.

The dropshot should never be attempted from near the baseline, and the backswing should be short and deliberate. What you are trying to do with the dropshot is to place it just barely over the net. If you try to hit the dropshot from the baseline, you not only have a difficult angle, you also give your opponent more time to read what you are doing and to get to the ball. The dropshot should always be hit from near the service line, or even closer to the net. Since you are close to the net, you have less time to prepare—therefore the shorter backswing.

Your body, if possible, should be side-on to the net, just as it is for the regular groundstrokes. Keep your eye on the ball as it comes

The dropshot should never be attempted near the baseline. The backswing should be short and deliberate. Try to place the ball barely over the net.

to you. The racket face should be open—that is, tilted upward—as you make contact with the ball. The racket comes under the ball as you swing; this imparts underspin to the ball. The swing itself is at about half the speed of the normal groundstroke.

The follow-through in the dropshot is also somewhat different from the groundstroke follow-through. In the groundstrokes, the follow-through is more or less across the body. In the dropshot, the follow-through should be along the flight of the ball. And this is very important: Hit through the ball. Keep the racket face open to impart underspin and hit through the ball. For some reason, just as with lobs, a lot of players seem half-hearted about hitting dropshots. Perhaps they think that because it's a soft shot, they needn't stroke the ball. This simply isn't true. Decide what you're going to do with the ball and then do it. Dropshots that are slapped or poked or hit half-heartedly wind up in the net more often than not.

The dropshot should clear the net by only, say, 12 or 18 inches. If you try to cut it any closer than that you're going to make too many errors. On the other hand, if the dropshot is going to go too deep into the opponent's court, then you're better off not to hit it. If you hit your dropshot too deep and your opponent gets to it, she's simply going to cream it for a winner.

Personally, I like to aim my dropshots for the short backhand area. I find that this is the easiest spot for me to hit to, since I don't

The follow-through in the dropshot is along the
flight of the ball. You must follow through.
Dropshots that are slapped, poked, or hit half-heartedly
wind up in the net more often than not.

Here I've hit the perfect dropshot. My
follow-through is aggressive and along the line of
flight. The ball appears to be high coming
over the net (opposite bottom left) *only*
because of the camera angle. The ball drops
close to the net near the backhand line.

have to bring the ball back across in front of my body. Also, I feel that this is one of the harder shots for my opponent to return. Even if she does manage to get to the ball, she's not going to be able to do much with it if she has to dig it out with her backhand.

I'm talking here, of course, about the forehand dropshot. The forehand and the backhand dropshot are hit in the same manner and are equally effective, but I myself find the forehand version much easier to control. Although there are a few players who can consistently hit good dropshots with their backhands, the most common variety by far is the forehand.

As I pointed out earlier, if you're playing on a fast surface, stay away from the dropshot altogether. On the other hand, when you're playing on a slow surface, use the dropshot quite often—at least once a game. The frequency with which you use the dropshot will depend, of course, on the amount of success you're having with it. If your opponent happens to be slow on her feet or if she is having trouble with it for any reason, you should use it as much as you can.

The dropshot has something in common with the lob, in that they both can incorporate the element of surprise. If your opponent has hit you a shot to the midcourt area and is out of position, she's going to be scrambling to get back to the center of the baseline. This is the perfect time to catch her off guard with the dropshot. She's going to be moving in the

wrong direction, and unless she's exceptionally quick on her feet, there's no way that she's going to be able to reach the ball.

The dropshot and the lob can, in fact, be used as a combination. Let's say, for instance, you're playing against an opponent who plays well from the baseline and tends to stay there most of the time. It's quite obvious that she's happy there, that this is the kind of game she likes to play. It's your job, therefore, to make her do something she doesn't like doing. If you're playing on a relatively slow court, you can do this by hitting the dropshot. This forces

your opponent to come to the net, an area where, in this case, she undoubtedly feels uncomfortable. Then, follow your dropshot with a lob and take the net yourself. The next time she's playing at the baseline, hit another dropshot, forcing her to come to net, and then try a sharp passing shot.

To practice the dropshot, stand at midcourt and have someone hit to you. Don't bother practicing the dropshot from the baseline, since it's foolhardy to even attempt a dropshot from that position. Stand at midcourt and hit dropshot after dropshot. By repetition

you'll develop confidence and a feel for the shot. Your targets should be the net and sideline; remember to keep your shots shallow.

Let me once again emphasize the most important points: Hit under and through the ball, keeping the racket face open. Pick your target area and hit the ball to it. If possible, turn sideways to the net—but remember, it's not always possible to have perfect footwork. You can hit this shot quite nicely from an open stance if the rest of your execution is correct. Remember to take a short backswing, and follow through into the flight of the ball.

Knowing when to hit the dropshot is important. When the ball is hit deep to me, I return a normal shot (left top and bottom), *but when the ball lands near the service line* (right top and bottom), *I move in and make a killing dropshot.*

Court
Strategy
by Nancy Richey

You can have the superior shots—and
lose to a superior player.

Nancy Richey, born in 1942 in San Angelo, Texas, has, since 1960, been ranked among the top 10 U.S. women tennis players 16 times, a record she shares with Louise Brough.

In 1968, Nancy won the singles title in the French Open; in 1969, she took the Australian championship; in 1972, she was ranked number two in the United States. During her career, she has won a total of six U.S. Clay Court championships, setting a record for women's national championship play by scoring 33 consecutive victories in that event. Nancy has made nine appearances on the Wightman Cup team, and she and her brother Cliff could become the first brother-sister team ever to reach the tennis Hall of Fame. They appeared in the U.S. top 10 for nine years in a row.

At 5 feet 3 inches, Nancy is essentially a baseline player, but the power she generates from there is usually sufficient to thwart even the hardest charging net-rushers. Her concentration on court is total, and she has a complete understanding of the dynamics of the game.

She played as Nancy Gunter after her marriage to Kenneth Gunter in 1970. Now, however, she has reverted to her maiden name.

Even though the same basic strategy is used by both men and women tennis players, women players tend to emphasize a different area of tactics. Whereas men play serve and volley on virtually every point, women—with a few exceptions—prefer to build their points more slowly. On most points—and on most surfaces —girls will rally for a fairly long time, exchanging 10 or 15, sometimes even 20, cross-courts before one of them hits an approach shot and goes to the net.

Court strategy can be divided into two categories: serving strategy and receiving strategy. In either situation one basic rule applies: Keep your weight forward. Many players have a tendency to lean backward—a mistake that costs them mobility. It's relatively easy to backpedal when your weight is forward, but it's very difficult to move forward quickly when your weight is on your heels.

Although, as I've just said, women don't serve and volley a great deal, it's a good idea —especially when playing on a fast surface, to attempt to do so at least occasionally. When I'm planning to serve and volley, I try to hit my serve into the T formed by the center and back service lines. In other words, if my opponent is right-handed, I hit to her backhand side when I'm serving to the deuce court and to her forehand side when I'm serving to the ad court. Serving down the middle in this way is the safest serve because it cuts down the angle of the opponent's return.

After hitting the serve and following it

in, my position at net is about a yard or so left of the center line when serving to the deuce court and a yard or so to the right of it when serving to the ad court. I try to get as close to the net as possible yet far enough back to be able to cover the overhead. The distance from the net will vary with each individual player —it just depends on how quick you are on your feet, how quickly you can move back into position when your opponent attempts to lob over you.

When I serve down the middle to the deuce court and go to net, my opponent has three possible shots. She can try to hit cross-court, wide to my forehand, which is a difficult shot; she can hit a lob—and remember, experience will tell you how far you'll have to be from the net in order to get back for the overhead; or she can try to hit the ball down the line, the most likely possibility.

If the return of service is down the line, my best shot is a wide cross-court volley to her backhand. Since the aim here is to pull the opponent out of court, the shot will be most effective if it's a fairly short, rather than deep, cross-court that's sliding out away from her. Of course, you can't do this every time because eventually she's going to start covering it. You also have to be able to hit the ball back down the line. This is a place that calls for close observation and a little bit of instinct. After hitting several cross-court volleys, you should be aware of whether your opponent is beginning to move to her left after hitting her return

*Kerry Harris serves to my backhand corner
and correctly covers that side of her court
(preceding page and below). My percentage return
is cross-court, but I don't get the right angle
on the shot. She returns deep to the opposite side.
I'm now out of court, and my only shot is a deep lob.*

The best place to put up a lob is to one of the corners, preferably the backhand corner—but I do mean corner. I hit to the corner, and Margaret Court is put in an awkward position (left). *At right my angle is bad, and Margaret has a forehand smash for a winner* (below).

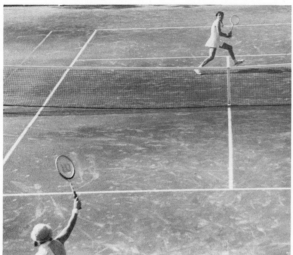

of service. The moment you notice that she is, you should hit a sharp volley down the line, catching her moving in the wrong direction.

If I serve down the middle to the deuce court and go to net and if my opponent hits her return cross-court to my forehand, I try to return a cross-court volley. The reason for this is that she is returning to center court; a sharply angled volley to her forehand side will force her to reverse direction and cover much more ground than would a down-the-line volley. Of course, whether or not I hit the volley cross-court depends a lot on how well she hits her return of service. If she has to slice up on the ball and her return is fairly high, I can hit the cross-court volley with little difficulty. If, on the other hand, she manages to hit a solid return that barely skims the net, I may be forced to dump it down the line and look for the winner on the next shot.

The third possible return when you're serving and volleying is the lob. Where you place your overhead depends on a lot of factors, but I would say that the best spot to aim for is your opponent's backhand corner. The secondary target in this case is the forehand corner. The variations in the placement of the overhead come as a result of your own instincts and the variations within your opponents themselves. If, for instance, your opponent has a weakness on one side or the other, you will naturally want to aim your overhead for her weaker side. Many players tend to hit a lob and then defend one side of the court or

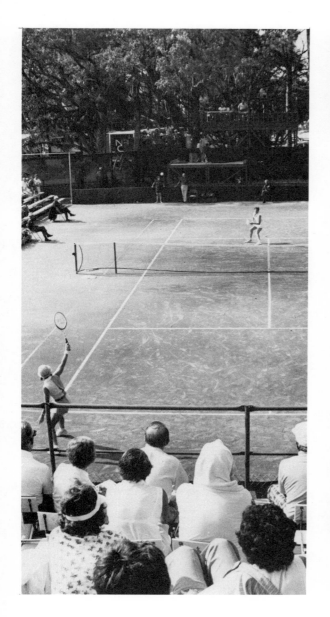

the other, just taking a chance that you'll hit the overhead to that side. In this case you'll naturally want to hit to the side of the court that is undefended.

If I should elect to serve wide—in the deuce court this would be to my opponent's forehand side—I will have given her a good angle for a sharp cross-court and also made it easier for her to hit down the line. So when you're serving and volleying, it's always best to serve for the T formed by the middle and back service lines.

If you want to vary your serve occasionally, aim for the center of the back service line, directly at your opponent. This not only will catch your opponent by surprise, but has the added advantage of being a difficult shot for most players to hit. This maneuver is particularly effective against tall, rangy girls, who can easily reach wide shots but who have difficulty getting out of the way of balls that are hit directly at them. Once again, when you're planning to serve and go directly to net, stay away from the wide serve—unless, of course, your serve is strong enough to pull your opponent so far out of court that she can't possibly make a good return.

Although I've been talking mainly about serving to the deuce court, or first court, the same basic strategy applies to the ad court—only, of course, reversed.

One of the fundamentals of court strategy is to keep your opponent always moving. Running your opponent serves at least two

When you come to net, it is often a good idea to serve down the middle, right at your opponent. Kerry Harris serves at me; I hit the ball right back at her; she draws me out of position and puts away a not-so-deep lob (left to right).

*Keep your opponent moving the wrong way.
My first volley pulls Kerry into the backhand
court, and my next volley draws her into
the forehand court* (top right). *She returns the
ball and heads back toward center court*
(bottom left). *I return to the forehand corner*
(bottom middle). *She gets the ball
and tries again to get back to center court.
Again I put the return in the opposite direction
from hers and catch her flat-footed.*

purposes. First, if you keep her moving right from the first point, she's naturally going to tire before long—each game she's going to be a little less quick, a little less powerful, a little less accurate in her timing, than she was the game before. Second, if you make your opponent travel the entire width or length of the court before hitting her shot, you've greatly increased the chances that she'll either make a weak return or miss the shot entirely. Once you've got your opponent moving, you want to make her reverse direction as often as possible—in other words, get her moving one way and then hit the ball the other. There are a number of combinations of shots that you can use to achieve these results.

For instance, say that you're exchanging cross-court forehands in a rally. Say that you hit 10 or 15 and then suddenly you hit one down the line to your opponent's backhand. If she should hit it back to your forehand instead of going cross-court—which is the logical shot —go back down the line. The logic behind this is simple. Your opponent has moved far to her left to return your first down-the-line shot. After she hits it, she'll be moving back toward center court to reposition herself. If you were to follow the natural impulse and return cross-court, it would be relatively easy for her to get to the ball, since she's already moving in the right direction. By going down the line the second time, you force her to stop suddenly and reverse direction—a maneuver that's both difficult and tiring.

*I've returned the ball low and shallow
to Margaret, giving her an opportunity to come to
net. She makes the correct approach shot—down
the line and hit with underspin.*

There's another tactic that you can use in the same situation. Again, you've been exchanging cross-court forehands. Say that you've hit 10 or 15 shots in a row to the same area of the court—the deep corner. On the next shot you look as though you're going to hit the ball to the same spot, but instead of hitting to the deep corner, you hit it on a short angle so that the ball strikes the court surface somewhere in the vicinity of the service line. This will pull your opponent out of court, and no matter what she hits you, you can then take the next shot and hit it out wide to her backhand. If you've executed the setup shot correctly, you'll have her so far out of position that there's no way she will be able to get to the second shot.

One of the times to be aggressive and take the net is when your opponent makes a miscue during a rally. For instance, you've once again been exchanging cross-court forehands and your opponent aims the ball for the deep corner but hits it short, say two or three feet past the service line. This is the time to attack. You should hit the ball down the line or to the deep middle—but still on her backhand side—and go in to the net. Your best approach shot is always down the line. The one exception to this rule occurs when your opponent hits a high, soft shot to your forehand side. In this case, you might be able to hit a sharp cross-court to win the point or to set up the winner on the next shot. If, however, your opponent hits the ball fairly low and with any kind of speed, stick to the down-the-line approach shot.

There is another basic rule of tennis strategy that explains the advantage of the down-the-line approach shot: You should always follow the flight of the ball into the net. If, in the situation we were just talking about, you hit a forehand shot down the line and follow it in, your position at net would be about a yard or so to the right of the center service line. If you hit the approach shot to the deep middle on your opponent's backhand side, your position can be almost exactly in the center of the net—and you have the added advantage of having cut down even more your opponent's angles for passing shots. In either position, you can easily cover the entire area of the net.

If, on the other hand, you try a cross-court forehand and follow it to net, you'll wind up a yard or two to the left of the center service line. And chances are that you won't even be able to reach your net position before your opponent hits the ball, since you have a much longer distance to travel. In the meantime, you've left her a lot of room to hit the cross-court—and if she does hit the cross-court, you'll have to reverse your direction on the dead run, which, as I've said before, is a very difficult move. By the same token, you've also given her a great angle for a down-the-line shot, a shot that will also be difficult for you to reach. Even if you do manage a return in this position, chances are that it will be so

weak that she'll be able to put the next shot away with little difficulty. Again, in almost all instances, hit your approach shot down the line or to the deep middle and follow the flight of the ball in to the net.

Hitting the ball to the deep middle of the court has another advantage that I might mention briefly. Most players are used to hitting the ball from wide angles. The center of the court is an area that most players don't use much; if you force them to hit from this position, their timing will often be thrown off and they will be forced into making mistakes. This tactic is especially useful against tall, rangy girls who, again, because of their longer arms and slower speeds have difficulty in coping with balls that are hit directly at them. It is also very effective against girls who are basically baseline players and win on wide shots.

Up to now, I've been talking mainly about strategy from the point of view of the server—although many of the points I've made apply to both serving and receiving. There are several rules that are important to follow when your opponent is serving. If, for example, your opponent is attempting to serve and volley, the foremost idea in your head should be to keep the ball as low as possible and still clear the net, no matter which side of the court you elect to return to. It's much more difficult to hit a good volley from a low position than it is from a high one. Usually, if you hit a good, low return, the volleyer will be forced to simply play the ball back safe. You'll then

have a really good opportunity to hit the passing shot. If, on the other hand, you hit the return high, the person coming to net is simply going to obliterate the ball. Remember, when you're receiving and the server is attempting to serve and volley, keep your return low.

During a point, if the server serves the ball and then stays back, the receiver should play the ball high—say five or six feet over the net—in order to utilize the depth of the

court. During a rally, you should be trying to make the ball constantly strike the court in an area that's within approximately three feet of the baseline. I can't emphasize enough the importance of this. The height at which you hit the ball will depend on the type of stroke you use and on how hard you hit, but most players will have to hit at the height I've already mentioned in order to keep the ball deep.

I myself prefer to hit the ball with top-

Françoise Dürr and I, both baseliners, know the importance of keeping the ball deep. In this rally, (left to right), we both stay deep, until she hits so deep that I set her up.

spin, for added control. It's not necessary to hit the ball with tremendous power—control and placement are much more important. Remember that it's much more difficult for your opponent to return even a fairly soft shot that lands near the baseline than it is for her to return a shot that's, say, 10 times harder but lands near the service line. If your opponent is at all competent and if your shots are consistently falling near the service line, well, to put it bluntly, you're going to get killed.

If, during a rally, you are hitting the ball high and deep but you suddenly miscue and hit one short, your opponent is probably going to take the opportunity to move to the net. This is the time to try to hit the ball hard and low over the net—skim the net tape if you can. Or, in certain instances, you might want to go for the soft, sharply angled shot. The main objective here is to do anything that will force your opponent to hit up on the ball. If you can force her to hit up, chances are good that she'll make a relatively weak volley, thus greatly improving your chances of winning the point with a passing shot or lob.

Remember that one of the most important aspects of tennis strategy is to do the unexpected as much as possible. Set a pattern and then suddenly vary from it, catching your opponent by surprise. Let's take an example. Let's say that during a match I've consistently been going for passing shots every time my opponent comes to the net. And let's say that she now makes an approach shot to my back-

I'm hitting the ball with topspin (above), *which I almost always do for added control.*
I've hit the ball shallow to Françoise (opposite top), *and she's taken the net* (bottom). *My only return now is to hit all out and try to force an error.*

173

hand and comes in to my backhand side. I know that she's going to position herself very close to the net because she's expecting the passing shot. Therefore it's time to lob. In this situation, my best lob is to her backhand corner. This forces her to move backward in an awkward position. It also forces her to cover more ground than would a lob to her forehand corner. If she had come to net on my forehand side, my best lob would still have been to her backhand corner. In this case, I could have made her run farther by hitting it to her forehand side, but the chances of her putting away a backhand overhead are much slimmer than they are of putting away a forehand overhead.

After hitting the lob, you normally want to get back to center court as quickly as possible to wait for the return. There are, of course, certain exceptions to this rule. If, for instance, you know where your particular opponent likes to hit certain shots, you will naturally cover the part of the court she normally hits to. In other cases, it's a matter of watching your own shot and watching your opponent to see what kind of shot she has decided to take. In the example we were just talking about, when you've hit a lob over her backhand side, you should watch to see whether she has elected to hit the backhand overhead. If she has, you should immediately move to cover your own backhand side since her easiest and most logical shot is a cross-court. It's extremely difficult to hit a backhand

Françoise comes to the net, and I lob. Although I haven't lobbed to her backhand, which I would have liked to do, my lob is deep, and unless she hits the short angle, I'll get to the ball.

overhead down the line. If she manages to do so, well, she wins the point, and she deserves to—but chances are she won't do it again.

Let's take another example of catching your opponent by surprise. Let's say you've been playing a match that's been marked by a lot of long rallies. In the course of these rallies, your opponent has miscued several times and hit the ball short, two or three feet past the service line, and each time you've smashed an approach shot and followed it to net. The next time she hits a short ball, instead of smashing it, dump a dropshot just over the net, either at a sharp angle to her forehand side or just down the line. Hopefully she will be playing back, looking for the hard approach shot, and won't be able to get to the ball. You should, however, follow your dropshot to net. If she does manage to get to the ball, she'll probably be able only to loop the ball up. No matter which direction she hits the ball, it should be a simple matter for you to put it away.

The kind of surface that you're playing on will, of course, affect your game strategy. When playing on grass, most players will serve and volley on almost every point. Since, on grass, the ball seldom bounces higher than thigh-high, your best position will be at the net. There are some women who will stay back and try to rally on grass, but if their opponent has any kind of net game at all, they will invariably lose. When the ball isn't bouncing up, it's next to impossible to hit good passing shots

As a baseliner, I've made the cardinal error—I returned Françoise's serve too shallow. She pounces on the ball with her backhand, drives me deep, and forces me to put up an easy lob.

175

with any kind of consistency. To repeat, when playing on grass, your best strategy is to serve and volley and hope that you can put together one good return game to break your opponent's serve and win the match.

On a medium-paced cement or asphalt court, you can serve and volley at least some of the time, depending on how strong your serve is. If your serve is very strong, you might even try to serve and volley on every point. If, however, you're playing against a good baseline player who has a good return of service, you may find that you're getting passed with regularity. In this case, it's better to stay back and wait until you get a short ball that you can use to start your attack.

On clay, there are very few women players who will attempt to serve and volley. Almost all the top women professionals prefer to stay back and work up their points more slowly when playing on clay. Of course, there are some clay courts that are almost as hard as asphalt or cement. On a very hard clay court, many women will, at least from time to time, attempt to serve and volley. On the average clay court, however, it's wisest to build your points from the baseline, waiting for your opponent to miscue and give you the opportunity to attack.

Knowing your opponent can be an invaluable aid in making tactical decisions on the court. If, as happens occasionally, I'm going to play someone I've never before played, I try to attend a match in which she's playing and study her style. I watch for weaknesses that I can exploit, as well as strengths that I should play away from, if possible.

But the most important things to watch for are patterns. Almost every player in the world has certain patterns of play; everyone has a favorite shot from a given position. For instance, there are players who, if you serve wide to their forehand, will 99 times out of 100 return down the line. Once you are aware of this, you can serve wide to her forehand and then immediately move to cover your backhand side.

Be especially alert during the early stages of a match. Watch for patterns and quirks and catalog them. Does your opponent prefer to play from the baseline or does she try to get to the net at every possible opportunity? If you take the net, does she prefer to lob or go for the passing shot? If you serve wide to her, does she return down the line or does she go for the cross-court? If you serve down the middle and go to net, will she try a lob followed by a passing shot or will she first try the passing shot and then the lob? Does she have trouble handling balls that are hit directly at her? Is she slower moving forward

It's tough to come to net on clay. Françoise drives me deep and comes to net (right and following page). But her approach shot hangs up on the slow surface, and I get to the ball. I then hit it in the opposite direction from hers, a basic rule of court strategy.

and backward than she is in her lateral movements, or vice versa?

Also, as I mentioned earlier, watch for your opponent's strengths. If she has an exceptionally good overhead, you'll be better off to keep your lobs to a minimum and go for the passing shots. If, on the other hand, your opponent is a better than average volleyer, you might want to go easy with the passing shots and rely more on lobs. The rule is very simple: If your opponent has one particular shot that is extremely potent, allow her to hit it as few times as possible.

Almost as important as knowing the pattern of your opponent's play is knowing the patterns of your own play. Try not to fall into unconscious patterns. If you are aware of your own patterns, you can set the pattern and then break it. Not only will breaking your patterns at strategic times win particular points for you, it will help you throughout the match, since your opponent will be unable to anticipate your placement on any shot.

When you're receiving serve, it's a good idea to try occasionally smashing the second serve as hard as you can and then following it in to net. If you can do this successfully, you will probably convince the server that her second serve is too weak. This will serve two purposes: First, she will probably try harder to get her first serve in—and normally the harder a player tries to get her first service in, the fewer times she is successful. Second, it will probably cause her to press harder on her second serve. Under these conditions, not only is your opponent likely to double-fault, but those serves that do go in are likely to be easier to handle.

If your opponent should hit a weak second serve to your backhand, run around your backhand, crack the ball hard with your forehand, and follow it in to net.

All points in a game are important, but some points are naturally more important than others. For instance, the first point is fairly crucial, but it's the second point of the game that you really want to win. If you've lost the first point, winning the second will pull you even—it's a brand new game. If, on the other hand, you've won the first point, winning the second will put you pretty well in control of the game at 30–0—losing it will put you right back where you started.

By the same token, if the score is 3–1 in games in a set, the next game in the set is extremely important. The difference between a set that is 3–2 and one that is 4–1 is huge, and if you happen to be the one who is trailing, you're faced with a long uphill battle.

If you happen to be down 0–30 and you're receiving serve, a cross-court is the safest shot to hit. In fact, whenever you're down game point, no matter what the situation, never hit a dropshot and never try for a screaming winner. Play it safe—keep hitting cross-courts and wait for your opponent to make a mistake. Remember, the time to be aggressive is when you're ahead.

Doubles
by Betty Stöve

Play the width, not the depth, keep smiling,
stay happy, and keep your partner for a friend.

Born in Rotterdam, The Netherlands, in 1945, Betty Stöve began her tennis career as a "ballboy." After a year of watching the top players from behind, Betty moved onto the court and began to develop her own game. Several times Dutch champion—in singles, doubles, and mixed doubles—she moved into the world top 10 in 1976 and has been there ever since.

In 1971, Betty was the only player other than Margaret Court to twice defeat Wimbledon and French champion Evonne Goolagong. In 1972, Betty defeated both Billie Jean King and Nancy Richey Gunter, then ranked numbers one and two in the world, as well as a number of other top-ranked players. Also in 1972, Betty became one of only four active women to win the grand slam of doubles. She combined with Billie Jean King to win the doubles titles at both Wimbledon and the French Championships, then teamed with Françoise Dürr to win the U.S. Open at Forest Hills.

At 5 feet 10 inches, Betty is one of the strongest women players in the world. Since 1976, she has finished second behind Chris Evert in the Colgate Series point standings for singles and first in doubles (1977); fifth in the Colgate Series Championships (1978); has won four titles on the 1979 Avon tour, including the Avon Championships doubles with partner Françoise Dürr; and won the 1979 U.S. Open doubles title with Wendy Turnbull.

To begin on an elementary level, doubles is a game of tennis played with four persons on the court—two on each side—all of whom belong to the same sex. In mixed doubles there are two players from each sex. Many women prefer doubles to mixed doubles because they feel that men hit the ball too hard and that the game is simply too competitive.

For these reasons, most women prefer to make their morning game of tennis a game of doubles—sometimes referred to as hit-and-giggle tennis. This may sound like an impolite term, but it isn't really meant to be. This type of tennis is meant to be enjoyable, and it's a good way for women to have fun and get their daily exercise. Singles tends to be more strenuous. You may find that an early morning match of singles will leave you too exhausted to cope with your responsibilities for the rest of the day.

Forming a partnership with your partner is very important in doubles. In a doubles partnership, it's almost crucial that there be sympathy and good understanding. If there is any sort of friction between the partners, then a mistake made by either is likely to cause ill feelings. Ill feelings in the partnership will cause you to lose matches, confidence, enjoyment—and your partner.

At one time there was a great deal of difference between the way that men played doubles and the way that women played doubles. Women used to stay at the baseline and engage in very long rallies—the ball was hit over the net perhaps 40 or 50 times on every point. Nowadays, however, men and women play basically the same game. Women's tennis, especially professional tennis, has become a much harder, faster game. It has become essentially a net game. If you want to play good tennis, whether men's or women's, you must come up to the net, get into position, and put the ball away with a volley.

It's very important that a doubles team be balanced. If there are two teams, one with a strong player and a weak player and one with two players of equal strengths, the team with equal strengths will almost invariably defeat the unbalanced team. The reason for this is obvious: If there is a weak player on the court, the opposing side is naturally going to play the ball to that weak player constantly.

Doubles is a game of strategy. Although the game is not played as hard as is singles, you have to use your head even more than in singles. In doubles it's necessary that you be alert, that you concentrate, and that you always keep optimistic. If you lose your optimism, you will become depressed when things go badly. And when you become depressed, you will, in turn, depress your partner. A depressed team is a losing team. Be happy on the court and always assume that you're going to win—even if your partner is, shall we say, less than a world-beater. Team spirit can help to make up for deficiencies in other departments.

If you plan to play doubles in a tournament and if you like to play on the left court, then look for a partner who likes to play on the right court. On the other hand, if you're happy on the right court, look for a partner who is happy on the left court. If you are equally happy on either side of the court, then obviously you have a much wider range of partners to choose from.

When looking for a tournament doubles partner, try to find someone who balances out your own game. If your own play is somewhat erratic, then look for a partner who plays a steady game. If you yourself are a steady player, then look for a partner who has a good volley and a good overhead. Before selecting a partner, you should take an objective inventory of your strengths and weaknesses and then find the partner who best complements you.

I've been talking mainly about developing a partnership for tournament tennis. If you're going to play just in a club, just for the fun of it, then it's a good idea to play with as many different partners as possible. You can do this quite easily by having a general sort of understanding, some common rules concerning what to do in given situations. If you're playing tennis for exercise and fun—and these are the reasons that most people play the game—never get mad at your partner (a rule that bears my repeating it). Tennis is a polite game, and it should always be fun—no matter what happens, keep smiling.

There are two basic positions in doubles. There is the parallel formation, in which both girls play at net or both girls play in back-

"Frankie" Dürr and I make a pretty fair doubles team. Not the least reason is team spirit. Here we're both in a good, ready position.

We receive in a balanced position, balanced
because we're more or less in the same position as are
our opponents, Kerry Reid and Kerry
Harris. Frankie's job is to return the
ball low over the net, preferably down the middle.

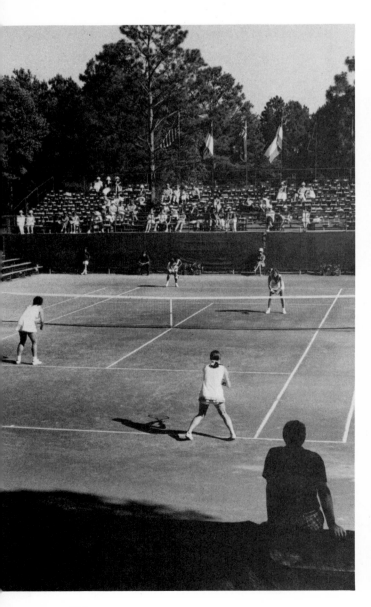
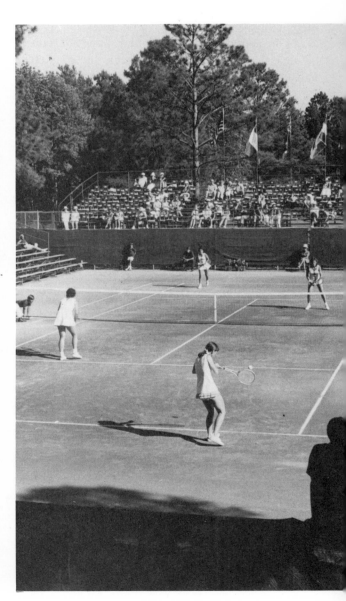

court. Then there is the unparallel position, in which one girl plays at net and the other at the baseline. Back in the 1940s, the style was for all four players to stay at the baseline. Then, as volleying became more popular, one player moved to the net. Today the common style is for all four players to play at the net. The result of this formation is a very quick—a sort of *tic-tac, tic-tac*—game.

Some weekend players will tend to stay in the backcourt, either because they are unsure of their volley or because they're a bit afraid of being hit by the ball. If you yourself have this tendency, you should try at all costs to overcome it. If you make the effort, you'll find that your confidence in your volley will increase rapidly. And, after you've been hit by the ball a few times, you'll realize that a tennis ball isn't all that hard. You'll have a much better chance of winning matches if both you and your partner come up to the net and play the smashes and volleys.

When you come to net, get as close in as possible. Try to avoid leaving open corners that will allow your opponents to exploit the wider angles of the doubles court. At the same time, always be aware of the threat down the middle of the court. Be alert, and be ready to move in either direction.

When playing against two net–rushers who come to net on every point, your best strategy is to hit a lot of high lobs and quick, loopy drives. These shots will force them to move back before they can again attempt to attack. In the meantime, you and your partner should be attacking.

There are two basic kinds of lobs—the offensive lob and the defensive lob. The offensive lob is hit, usually with topspin, just over the opponent at net. The attacking lob doesn't go as high as does the defensive; it's a much quicker shot and gives the opponent less time to get back for the return. The defensive lob, on the other hand, is usually hit quite high and with underspin. The object of the defensive lob is to give you and your partner time to get back into position when you've both been pulled out of court.

After hitting a defensive lob, you must wait to see what your opponents are going to do with it. If you see that your opponents are going to smash, then you have to stay back near the baseline. But if you see that your opponents are simply going to keep the ball in play, then you should try to take over the attack by coming in to net.

When you hit an attacking lob, you should always go with it—that is, follow your shot to the net and try to maintain the initiative. Your opponents will have a very difficult time trying to put away an offensive lob, and you should be sitting right on top of the net ready to make the kill.

When you don't know what to do with the ball, use the safe shots that we've already discussed. Hit the ball down the middle, hit a lob, stay away from dropshots, try to use the width of the court at all times, and avoid mak-

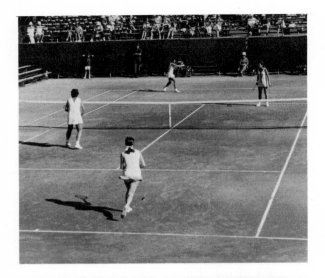

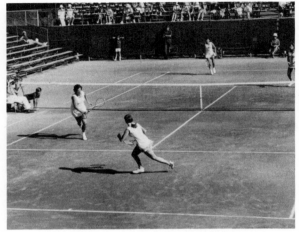

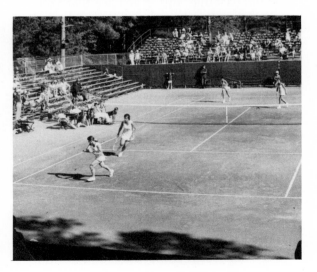

Kerry R. lobs over my head (left), *and when she sees that we're both going back for the ball, she joins her partner at net. The lob is an extremely effective shot in doubles. It opens up the court and forces your opponents out of position, as in the sequence at the right.*

ing silly mistakes. An example of a silly mistake in doubles is playing a dropshot. The dropshot should hardly ever be played in doubles because there is always one player in position near the net. From this position, she will have no trouble getting to the ball and drilling it away for a winner.

The lob, on the other hand, is a very good shot to play in doubles. You'll find that the lob is extremely effective in doubles because it causes the opposing side to switch over—that is, to exchange sides of the court. To change sides efficiently, the members of a team must have a very good understanding of each other. Even if a team does have this understanding, the lob still has the effect of breaking up their position, leaving holes in their defense. After hitting the lob and breaking up your opponents' position, you simply direct your volley or overhead into one of those holes.

Another basic rule in doubles is that the partner with the stronger serve should serve first. If, however, you are right-handed and your partner is left-handed, or vice versa, then arrange your serving order so that neither of you will have to look into the sun while serving. If, for instance, the sun is on your left, then you as the right-hander should serve. If both your opponents are right-handed, one of them will be looking into the sun when she serves, whereas neither you nor your partner will have to deal with this annoyance. It's a small advantage, but one that just might make the difference in a tight match.

You have the option of changing your serving order at the end of any set. If you should lose the first set, you might try reversing your order. Again, a small change such as this just might make the winning difference in a close match.

If you never rush the net after serving, your opponents don't have to be careful about how high they hit the return. If you do rush the net, you force your opponents to use caution and to look for the corners—you force them, in other words, to hit the difficult shots. And when you force your opponents to hit difficult shots, you force them to make mistakes.

Variation is also very important in the game. You shouldn't, therefore, rush the net behind every serve. Rush sometimes, stay back sometimes—and vary the rest of your attack in such a way that you never establish a predictable pattern. Keep your opponents guessing.

If you are able to play the various kinds of serves—the flat, the slice, the twist—you should mix up your serves as well. This same principle applies to return of service. Keep your opponents in a situation in which they have to be expecting almost anything at almost any time. Lob often, play cross-courts, play hard shots, play soft shots. Never let your opponents read your game, and surprise them as often as possible. Your objective at all times should be to make your opponents play a more difficult shot than the one that you just played to them. Play the easy shots and let your opponents make the mistakes. Remember, if you

don't make any mistakes, then you can't lose.

The serving position in doubles is somewhat different from the serving position normally used in singles. In singles, most players stand about two feet or a yard from the center line. In doubles, your position should be about midway between the center line and the first sideline. If you stand too near the center line in doubles, your opponent will simply hit a sharply angled cross-court that will be impossible for you to reach. By standing nearer the sideline, you should be able to cover this exposed area of the court. This applies to either side of the court.

To find the correct net position for doubles, stand about one yard from the outside service line. Stand so that when you extend your racket, you can just touch the net. Now take one step backward. This is the position you should be in when your partner is serving—about one yard from the outside service line and about a yard and a half from the net. From this position you should be able to cover the down-the-line passing shot as well as the center area of the net.

When you're receiving serve, try to stand in the line that you expect the serve to follow. If the server moves to her right, then you should move to your right; if she moves to her left, move to your left. By balancing out your opponent's movements and staying on a line with her, you can help avoid unpleasant surprises on the serve.

You should have a good first serve that is

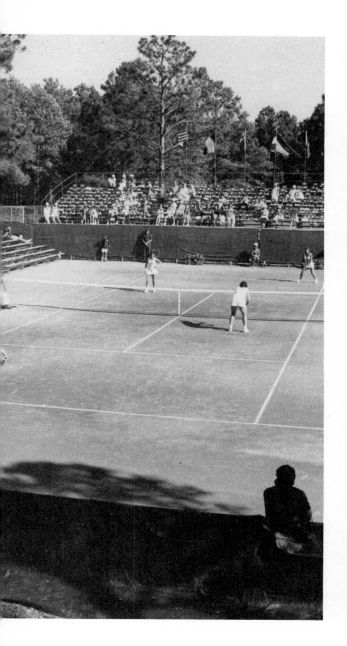

The server's position is different in doubles.
She lines up close to the
halfway mark between the service
mark and the singles sideline. The woman
at net should be about a yard from the outside
service line and about four feet from the net.

consistently going in. If your partner knows that the first serve is going to be in and knows what area of the service court you're aiming for, she'll be able to handle her responsibilities confidently and efficiently. If your serve is inconsistent, your net game will be greatly weakened. Get your first service into court, even if it means easing off from your normal pace. Then get in as close to the net as possible for the first volley.

It's equally important that you have a good, consistent return of service. Your partner should know what you are going to do with your return, and she should be confident that you are going to do it well. I play a lot of doubles with Françoise Dürr, and she hits a lot of lobs on return of service. I know exactly when she's going to hit the lob, when she's going to cross over, and so on. When you've developed a partnership to this level, you'll get a feeling of great satisfaction.

Keep your vocal interchanges on court as short as possible. You need say only enough to let your partner know what you intend to do. If, for example, you've been lobbed over, shout either "yours" or "mine" to let your partner know whether or not you can get to the ball. The more quickly you can indicate your intentions to your partner, the more time she'll have to get into proper position. Let your partner know your plans as early as possible, and tell her in the most concise manner you can. "I don't believe I can quite get to this particular shot, so perhaps you had better take it" is a very polite statement, but it's not exactly the epitome of efficiency.

Crossovers—also called switchovers or poaches—are a basic tactic in doubles. Crossovers can be executed both when your team is serving and when your team is receiving. Let's say that my partner is serving. She hits in a good first serve. I know in advance which area of the court she is aiming for, and therefore I know that the receiver will probably return the ball on only a certain angle. The moment the receiver begins her return, I quickly move laterally along the net, hoping to pick off the return with a winning volley. In the meantime, my partner is also moving laterally, moving to cover the area that I have just vacated.

The crossover maneuver is basically the same when your side is receiving. Let's say that I'm receiving serve in the right, or forehand, court. On the return of service, I'll try to hit a sharp cross-court. My partner knows where my return is going, so she has a good idea of what the server will try to do with it. The moment the server's racket touches the ball for a return, my partner will begin to move to her right to a position from which she can hit the winning volley. Simultaneously, I'll be moving to my left to cover the alley in the event that the server has intuited the crossover and hit a shot down the line.

Never move on the crossover before your opponent has hit the ball. If you move too soon, your opponent will guess your intention and hit the ball down the alley. Move just as

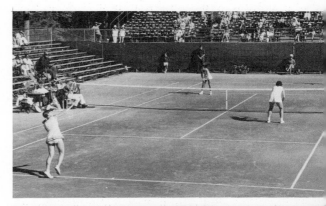

As you can see from this sequence (left to right), *it's important that both partners be able to hit the overhead. You don't have to have a killing overhead, but you must keep the ball in play and go for the angles.*

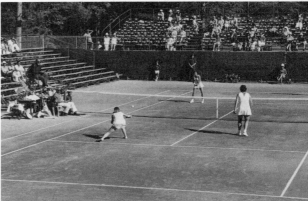

she hits the ball, when she is already committed. The crossover maneuver should always be a surprise to your opponents.

The crossover is a good tactic to use on important points. But whenever you use the crossover, be sure to go all the way. Don't stop in the middle and leave your partner hopping up and down on the baseline trying to cover both sides of the court. Admittedly, crossovers are a bit of a gamble. Sometimes you'll get caught and lose the point. But if executed properly—and this is where teamwork really pays off—crossovers will win more points than they lose.

The better player of a partnership should play in the left-hand, or backhand, court as much as possible. The reason for this is that a lot of balls come straight down the middle in doubles, and it's usually best that the player on the left take these balls with the forehand.

But even more important than the down-the-middle shots are the lobs. If you and your partner are relatively equal as players, then the one who has the better overhead should take the backhand court. As I've already mentioned, the lob plays an important part in doubles, and a great many lobs are hit during the course of a match—most of them to the backhand court. It's very important, therefore, that the person playing the backhand side of the court be able to smash the lob away, or at least keep the ball in play. If you can consistently turn your opponents' lobs into winners, your net game will be greatly strengthened—

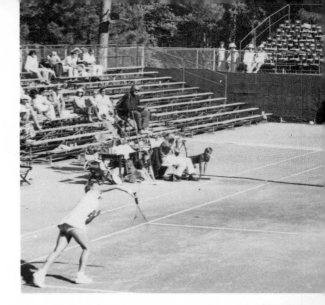

and the net game is very important in doubles.

The middle of the court is important in doubles from both an offensive and defensive point of view. First of all, there must be a good understanding between you and your partner as to who will take the balls that come right down the center line. If you and your partner are hesitant as to who is going to take the shot, the ball may pass between you untouched while you stand there looking at each other. Or, even worse, the match may be brought to a premature ending by a head-on collision. After you have played with a particular partner for a while, this understanding will develop. When playing with a partner for the first time, it's a good idea to have a prematch conference to determine exactly how to handle this situation. You might decide that the person playing the backhand court will take all down-the-middle shots with her forehand. Or you might to decide to rely on signals—the "mine" or "yours" that we talked about earlier.

Often this situation will be resolved by the fact that one partner is more involved in the point than the other. If, for instance, your partner has hit the last two shots and seems to be tuned in to the point, it is usually better to allow her to take the shot that comes down the middle, even though you may feel that you have a slightly better angle or position. Of course, it's then up to your partner to make the same concession when the situation is reversed. Split-second decisions such as this are best made when you know your partner well.

In doubles you play the width of the court, not the depth. Because of this, it's often best to serve at your opponent. Kerry H. serves wide to my backhand (below), but I'm able to make good use of the angle in my return.

If you're unfamiliar with your partner's style of play, it's generally best to work out a firm understanding and not deviate from it.

Whereas in singles you play the depth of the court, in doubles you should play the width of the court. You want to hit the wide-angle shots that will force your opponents to hit up on the ball. If you can play these shots, you'll force your opponents to make mistakes—to either hit the ball into the net or hit an easy setup that you can kill off with a volley or overhead.

You can also use the middle offensively. The middle in doubles is a weak point. If your opponents aren't used to playing with each other, it's a good idea to hit down the middle as much as possible. Even if your opponents have been playing together for a long time, it's still a good idea to send the ball down the middle fairly often. Even an experienced doubles team can get confused, and the slightest bit of hesitation can mean the difference between winning and losing the point.

The move to the net after receiving serve is actually a two-part move. After hitting the return, you should sprint about four strides forward. A couple of feet before the service line, you should slow up. What you are doing is taking a small stutter step as your opponent strikes the ball. You don't stop your forward movement, but at the same time, you don't continue to rush headlong toward the net. In this way you're ready to move in any direction for the volley. After the receiver has hit the return

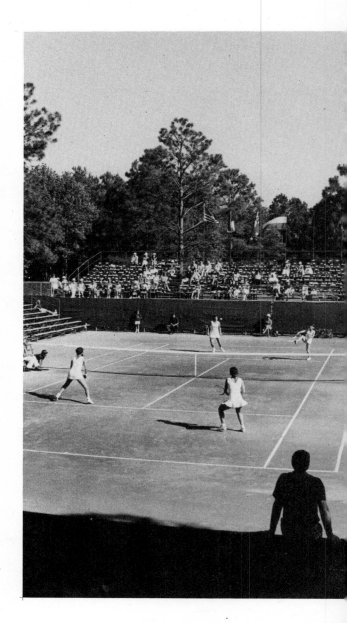

Exploiting the angles and the width of the court are your objectives even when you're hitting an overhead. Instead of smashing the ball, Frankie actually passes Kerry H. on an overhead.

Even against players who are used to each other, it's a good idea to play down the middle (left). *Here I force Kerry R. to hit up, a shot that I easily put away. Kerry H. tries to vary the expected cross-court return by hitting down the line* (right), *a good piece of strategy.*

and you see its direction, you should immediately move to intercept the flight of the ball. You should be able to reach the ball in two strides, and when you hit the volley, you will still be moving forward toward the net. By not committing yourself until after your opponent has hit the ball, you can better cover your half of the court. If you try to go to the net in one headlong rush, you'll find that you're being passed or lobbed with consistency. On your way to the net, never lose sight of the ball.

The best return of service in doubles is usually cross-court. Of course, if you consistently hit cross-courts on return of serve, sooner or later your opponents are going to get used to your system and develop a rhythm. The best way to break this rhythm is to hit a good attacking lob over the net player. An especially good time to do this is at 30–all or at game point. In tense moments such as these many players seem to have difficulty getting their arms up; they tend to get a little too much elbow into their overheads.

There are many important aspects to doubles, but the most important, once again, is team spirit. Remember that tennis is, after all, just a game and that you're out there to have fun. Never get angry or upset with your partner. Encourage her, congratulate her on her good shots, commiserate with her on her bad ones. Keep happy, keep smiling, and keep your partner for a friend.

Mixed Doubles
by Françoise Dürr

Play position, think middle, understand
your partner, and don't be afraid to play to the
woman opponent.

"She does everything wrong right," the photographer for this book observed of Françoise Dürr. Born on Christmas Day, 1942, in Algiers, Frankie began teaching herself tennis at the age of 13. When, at the age of 18, she acquired her first coach, the coach decided that it was best not to try to change her style—a decision that, looking at Françoise's record, was obviously a correct one. Her style is, to use her word, unique—it's also effective.

At 5 feet 4 inches, 120 pounds, even with her "unique" style, Frankie hits the ball well and is an exceptional singles player. Married in 1975 to Boyd Browning, a TV-radio executive, Françoise has been ranked as high as third in the world (1967) and has ranked six times in the world's top 10 singles list.

But her true forte is doubles. She won the French Open doubles title for five years running. She has also won twice at the U.S. Open—once with Darlene Hard and once with Betty Stöve—and has won virtually every other major doubles and mixed doubles title in the world. A runner-up in Wimbledon doubles six times, in 1977 she teamed with Virginia Wade to reach the finals of the Bridgestone Championships and won the Colgate Championships final. Also with Betty Stöve, she won the 1979 Avon Championships doubles.

In mixed doubles, the man is normally the stronger player. As such, he should take all the more difficult shots—he should hit the majority of the overheads and do the majority of the poaching, or crossing over. On the other side of the coin, the weakest point of the opposing team is normally the woman. Therefore, when playing mixed doubles, you should try to play the ball to the woman opponent as much as possible. For instance, it's usually much easier to lob over the woman than it is the man simply because the man almost always has extra height and reach. Naturally, from time to time, you'll face a mixed doubles team in which the woman is a stronger player than her partner. In this case, you should do the contrary—in other words, you should always play to the weaker opponent.

When playing mixed doubles, I don't think you should have any compunctions about playing to the woman partner of the opposing team. Many men feel that they shouldn't serve a big serve or hit a hard volley to a woman, and a lot of women feel guilty about playing the majority of their shots to the woman. I think this is silly. If a woman is on the court, it means that she wants to play and is willing to take her risks. It's really more unfair and unsportsmanlike not to play the ball to her. In mixed doubles, it's an accepted rule that you play the ball to the weaker player—which is usually the woman. Most women are willing to admit that men are bigger and stronger—it's a fact of life. If you take it easy on your

Generally in mixed doubles, it's a good
idea to play to the woman. Here, I return Kathy
Kemper's serve in the form of a lob to her partner,
Walter Troutman. Walter puts it away. In the sequence
on the following pages, I lob Kathy. This time
it works,and they are both out of position.

female opponent and don't try all-out to win, she should be insulted.

Mixed doubles, as well as regular doubles, is a very different game from singles. For one thing, power is not as important. Doubles is a game of angles, finesse, and teamwork. If you look at the records of top players, you'll notice that many players have done well in singles but have never excelled in doubles. Some players, on the other hand, have won a lot of doubles titles but have seldom gotten to even the quarterfinals in singles. I myself am a case in point. I've won every major doubles title in the world—with the exception of Wimbledon, where I've been in the finals five times —most of them several times. But if you examine my singles record, you'll find it's not so impressive.

The volley is also different in doubles. In singles you have a lot of territory to cover once you get to the net, and unless you have a very strong serve to follow in and are very fast, you're going to get passed fairly often. In doubles you have your partner to help you out, and the doubles court being wider than the singles court, you have only a little more than half the court to cover. And because the court is wider in doubles, you can hit your volleys on much sharper angles.

Basically, the net game is much easier to play in doubles. When I'm playing doubles, I'll go to the net at any time. In my singles game, on the other hand, I won't go to the net unless I'm forced to, unless my game isn't

working and I feel I have to try something different. In doubles I'll go to the net without hesitation, and I find that I play at the net most of the time.

Again, power is not as important in doubles as it is in singles. A lot of people when playing doubles will try to hit the overhead or the volley as hard as they can. This is a mistake. Hit the ball into a deep corner, or hit it on a sharp angle. Hitting the ball with all your might in doubles is a waste of energy—and causes you to make mistakes.

The most important aspect of doubles is teamwork. A lot of people have the attitude of, well, you play your side of the court and I'll play mine—but this doesn't work. You've got to be keyed in to your partner at all times. Every time you hit a shot, you should be aware of where your partner is on the court, what your partner is doing, and how your shot will affect your partner.

Always remember that you and your partner are a team. When your partner makes a mistake, don't say, "Oh! How can you miss a shot like that?" Instead, say "Bad luck" or "Good try." Don't put added pressure on your partner—it's the worst thing you can do. I remember the first time I played mixed doubles with Pancho Gonzalez. I was shaking all over. I said to myself, "Oh-yi-yi, what can I do? What's he going to say, especially when he sees my funny game, my funny grip?" But Pancho said, "Come on now, don't be scared just because you're playing with me. Do the best you

When coming to net after serving, you come to the side of the center service line. The volleying position is just inside the service line.

can and I won't yell at you." He put me so at ease that I was able to play my best, and we won. Keeping happy and keeping your partner happy will not only allow you to enjoy the game more, it will help you to win.

Position is very important in doubles. For many, many years, and even today—unless you're playing at the very top professional level—the normal position has been for one partner to play at the net and the other to play back near the baseline. On the top professional level you'll often see all four players positioned at net. I think, though, for the beginner, and even for the fairly advanced weekend player, it might be better to stay with the one up, one back formation.

Always try to have the same position that your opponents have. If they have one at the net and one in backcourt, then you should have one at net and one in backcourt. When they're both at net, both you and your partner should be at net. As much as possible, keep the positions balanced. When your position becomes unbalanced, you leave holes in your defense. Your opponents will quickly notice these holes and begin to exploit them.

As in regular doubles, you should have some basic understandings with your partner before you go onto the court. One of the things you should discuss before the match is who will take the shot that comes down the middle. Normally the partner who has the ball on the forehand side—usually the man since he normally will play in the backhand court—

will take this shot, but there are many ways to work out this problem, depending on your style of play and your partner's style of play. The important thing is that you have a firm understanding so that you can avoid confusion and hesitation on the court.

In mixed doubles the middle of the court is very important. You should concentrate on defending your own middle, and you should try to attack the middle of your opponents' court as much as possible. By this I don't mean that you should ignore the alleys—they're also important. Doubles is a game of sharp angles, and your opponents will be trying for the sharp shots to the corner and the down-the-line passing shots—but these shots are much more difficult for your opponents to hit. Occasionally your opponents will hit a good shot down the alley for a winner. Don't let this disturb you. Just say to yourself, "Too good, good luck, let's see you do that again."

I've said that the man (provided he is the stronger partner, of course) should do most of the poaching, or crossing over. This doesn't mean that you should never try to poach. I think it's a bit easier to poach when your partner is serving than it is when your partner is receiving serve. If your partner hits a good serve and you think you have a chance to pick off the return with a volley, then try it. The important thing to remember when crossing over is to commit yourself all the way. You must decide to go and then go all the way. Your partner is watching you, and when you

When executing the crossover, the person at net
waits until the last moment, then crosses all the
way. He can't hesitate and can't stop. The
server should be able to see her partner crossing
and should then cross over herself to cover the
empty court. This double crossover becomes
much easier after you've been playing together awhile.

start to cross, he'll start to cross the other way. If you go halfway and stop, you'll both be stuck in the same position and there will be big holes on either side of the court.

Wait until the return of serve has been hit before you start to move on the crossover. For one thing if you move too soon, your opponent will pick up the movement and drive the ball down the alley. Another reason to wait is to see what the receiver decides to do with the ball. Also, you can usually tell by the way the receiver hits the ball whether or not you'll be able to reach it.

One good reason you must wait to see what the receiver is going to do with his shot before you poach is that he might lob. If your opponent lobs over you and you haven't poached, you'll be in position to possibly hit an overhead. If the lob is too good, your partner might take the shot, in which case you'll switch courts. Having gone back for the lob initially you'll be in position to accomplish the switch easily.

But suppose you poach too early and the receiver throws up a lob. If he lobs over the area you just left, your partner will be able to take the shot, but you'll be stuck at net. And if he lobs to the position just vacated by your partner, then neither of you will be in position to take the shot! So cross at the right time, and when you decide to cross, forget about caution and just go. If you miss it, you miss it.

The crossover is a difficult move for beginners, but because it is such a basic tactic in

Here is a good example of badly played
mixed doubles. My partner has served and has elected
to stay at the baseline, which is all right
since he feels more comfortable there. But when I cross
over, he doesn't, leaving the court open.

doubles, I recommend that beginners attempt it from the very start. You may miss a lot in the beginning, but each time you try the poach, it will come a bit more naturally. Eventually, after enough tries, you'll be able to execute the poach with confidence.

If your opponents are poaching a great deal and are being successful at it, try to hit a few hard returns down the alley. This is a difficult shot and not really a high percentage shot, but even if you miss, you've served a purpose. As long as your opponents know that you're willing to attempt the passing shot down the alley, they will be a little more conscious of the possibility of being passed and a little more reluctant to try the poach. In tennis, a hesitation of a split second can make a great deal of difference.

When playing at net, your position—when your partner is serving—should be two or three feet from the sideline and a yard or two from the net. *The distance between you and the net is crucial.* If you play too close to the net, then it will be easy for your opponents to lob over you. On the other hand, if you are too far from the net, then your opponents will be able to slam the ball directly at your feet—a shot that is almost impossible to return.

When you are at net and your partner is receiving serve, your eyes should be on the opponent who is at net. Don't bother watching the server or your partner—you should know what your partner is going to do in any event. If you are watching your opponent at net, you

should usually be able to detect a poach attempt in its early stages. If you are alert enough and quick enough, you'll be able to get yourself ready to intercept the poach and save the point.

A lot of beginners and weekend players don't like to play at the net. They are a little bit frightened and uncomfortable at the net, and therefore they don't play well in that position. I think that if you like to play in the backcourt, then you should play in the backcourt. Simply tell your partner that you feel uncomfortable at the net and prefer to stay back. Then it's just a matter of his taking the net position every time and your moving to backcourt every time.

In doubles, it's very important that you get your first serve in. It's not so important that the serve be a powerful one. Hit the first service deep and be sure that it goes in. This will give you time to get to the net if you want to or to get into position near the baseline if you prefer. It will also help your partner if he can be relatively certain that the first serve will go in.

Normally the man leads off the serving order. This rule is not always followed on days when there is a wind blowing the length of the court. It is customary for the woman to serve with the wind. This will add pace to her serve and will help her with the first volley when coming to net.

When you're serving and your partner poaches, you should immediately move to

cover the side of the court he has just left—either going to the net or staying back on the side, depending on your preference and quickness. If he is successful with the poach, chances are the point will be over. If he is only partially successful—if he hits the ball but fails to put it away—you may have to play a return. If he misses the poach, there's very little you can do about it. Once you and your partner have made the switch, it's important that you both stay where you are. Don't try to switch back on the next shot. It doesn't matter which side of the court you are on, as long as the entire court is defensed.

When going to net from backcourt, you should always try to get past the service line. The area between the baseline and the service line should be avoided as much as possible. This area is no-man's land. When you are in this area, almost anything your opponents hit to you will be difficult to return. If you manage to get the ball back at all, chances are that you'll put the ball up in the air, giving your opponents an easy put-away. If you're going to stay back, stay within a foot of either side of the baseline. If you're coming to net, get inside the service line. Avoid the middle area.

You should talk a lot to your partner, especially if things aren't going well, first to encourage him and also to see whether you can't work out a better strategy. For instance, some days one player might have a forehand that's not working. You and your partner should have a talk between games and try to

*On the preceding pages, Kathy Kuykendall returns
serve to me. No matter how far over Pete
comes, I can still angle the ball well enough so that I
don't have to worry about him. It's important not to get
caught in the middle of the court (left).
During a rally, Pete comes too far in from the
baseline (to no-man's land). I hit a
volley at his feet, and he returns high to
my partner, Howard Hunt, who puts the shot away.*

*The effectiveness of the lob volley: During
a net rally, Kathy hits to Howard* (top left),
who returns to Pete (top right). *Pete returns to
me* (middle left). *The shot is a good one—low
and down the line* (middle right). *This is the
time to throw up a lob volley. It makes a
very difficult return for Kathy* (bottom right).

work out a plan to make up for this deficiency.
It might be as simple as switching courts.

Other times, more specific tactical changes
may improve your game. For instance, say
I've been going to net when I serve to the
woman on the opposing side but staying back
when I serve to the man. This is a fairly common tactic. If, however, the man is very good
at the dropshot, he will simply hit a sharply
angled cross-court dropshot off my serve. If he
has done this several times and if each time
I've been unable to get to the ball—or have
gotten to it but been unable to do anything
with it—I'll warn my partner and then rush
the net the next time I serve to the man. If
he again tries the dropshot, I'll be in position
to hit an easy winner. Even if he doesn't try
the dropshot, chances are he'll be so surprised
that my side will win the point anyway.

If every time you serve to the man in the
ad court, he overpowers you with his return of
serve to your backhand, talk to your partner
and suggest trying the Australian tandem. This
is a doubles style seldom seen in this country,
but my partners and I have used it many times
with great success. It has a way of confusing
the opposition.

In the Australian tandem your partner,
rather than standing in the opposite court from
you, stands in the same court. In other words,
if you're serving to the ad court, he'll be standing in the backhand court, whereas normally

224

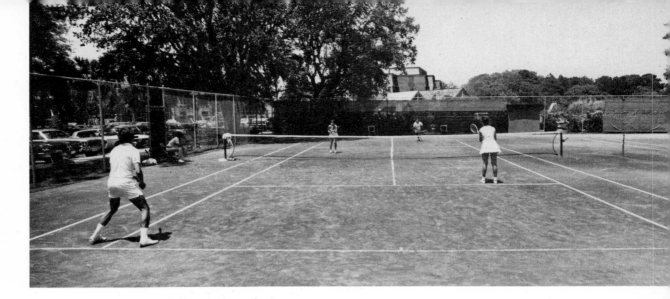

he would be standing in the forehand court. The man on the opposing team has become accustomed to hitting sharp cross-courts to your backhand. Now if he hits cross-court, he'll hit directly to your partner at net—and very often, either because he is confused, hasn't been paying attention, or is simply in a groove, he'll do just that. Even if he does notice the change, he'll have to hit a shot that he's not used to hitting—either a lob or a drive down the line to my forehand.

Switching to the Australian tandem in the middle of a match breaks up your opponents' rhythm and forces them out of the groove they have gotten into. It forces them to find a completely new strategy. While your opponents, hopefully confused and demoralized, are regrouping, you and your partner should be piling up points and games.

It is possible to rush the net after serving in the Australian tandem, but I would advise the weekend player to stay at the baseline.

After losing a match, wait 10 or 15 minutes before discussing the match with your

head. Howard can't cover because he's already crossed, and I'm in an awkward position to go back.

partner. After a short cooling-off period, the two of you are much more likely to be objective and to be able to make constructive tactical plans for the future.

Let me give some final words of advice concerning mixed doubles. First of all, I think to preserve off-court harmony that it's perhaps better not to play mixed doubles with your husband or boyfriend for a partner. Most couples tend to criticize each other, and on-court bitterness can ruin more than a match.

Next, when playing mixed doubles, re-member that a man's on-court ego is more likely to be affected than yours. If he wants, let him take the difficult shots, especially if he can do a better job than you anyway. Sometimes you may make an exceptional shot and set up a winner that your partner then puts away. You may feel he gets too much credit for this, but this is the way the game should be played. Expect it and accept it.

Finally, a word to the men: If you're playing tennis with a beautiful lady, try to keep your eye on the ball.

Physical Fitness and Equipment

by Kerry Harris

Keeping fit will not only help you to avoid injuries, it will increase your enjoyment as it improves your play.

Born in Melbourne, Australia, in 1949, Kerry Harris began playing tennis at the age of 10. As is common in Australia, her first instructors were her parents. She was quickly sidelined by osteomyelitis, a bone infection, but by the age of 13 had overcome it and was back on the court.

In 1970, dissatisfied with her rate of development, she began to see Merv Rose, a teaching pro, in an attempt to improve and simplify her game. By 1971, she had radically changed her style and was showing improvement in tournament play. She reached the quarterfinals of both the South African Open and the U.S. Clay Court. In 1972, she reached the semifinals of the Australian Open. In 1973, Kerry for the first time reached the finals of a Virginia Slims event, defeating Nancy Richey along the way, also a first for Kerry.

At 5 feet 7½ inches, Kerry had a tremendously powerful first serve and all the shots to go with it. In this chapter Kerry talks about the grind of the pro tour and about the importance of physical fitness. "I like to keep fit all the time," says Kerry. "But I'm like anyone else. If we have an off week, I like to have a bit of a lash-out."

Kerry retired from competitive tennis in 1975, when she married. She now lives in Australia.

Being physically fit greatly reduces the chances of your incurring an injury while playing tennis. Moreover, if you should happen to sustain an injury, being physically fit will help you to recover quickly and completely. And, needless to say, your degree of fitness will often affect the outcome of a match —especially a long one.

Physical fitness is, of course, much more important to the professional tennis player than it is to the weekend player. The pro tour is really a grind, and you have to be in top condition to keep up with it. You're traveling to a different city every week, playing match after match, sometimes late at night, sometimes early in the morning. Sleeping in a different bed every week and living out of a suitcase almost all year round is alone enough to wear you down. Unlike other occupations, you have to be in top shape to do your job. A pulled muscle or a cold costs you money.

To the weekend player, on the other hand, one of the attractions of tennis is that it offers the opportunity to exercise. For many women, playing tennis is the only chance they have to tone their muscles and maintain a degree of fitness. All the same, if you wind up injuring yourself or becoming ill because you haven't prepared properly or taken care of yourself properly, then you're defeating your purpose.

Exactly how much attention you pay to physical fitness depends largely on how seriously you take your game. If you play merely for fun and exercise, then you need use only a bit of caution. If, however, you take your game more seriously, if you want to excel in competitive tennis, perhaps even become a professional, then you're going to have to spend a lot of time and effort conditioning yourself. To develop the stamina and agility necessary to play top-level tennis takes discipline and many hours of hard work. If you are really serious about tennis, I suggest that you put yourself under the guidance of a professional trainer or coach. A trainer or coach can outline an extensive program for you, tailored to your specific needs.

When I was 16 years old and had been playing a few years, I was lucky enough to work with Stan Nichols, one of the top Australian trainers. Stan had me on an intensive program to develop strength, stamina, and agility. I worked outdoors—jogging, sprinting, and so forth—as well as in the gymnasium, where I did exercises such as skipping rope, lifting weights, doing sit-ups and push-ups. Stan also gave me guidance with my diet. When you are training seriously and trying to build yourself up, it's especially important to eat a well-balanced, nutritious diet.

For the beginner, or for the weekend player who is starting in after a layoff, the important thing is to begin slowly. For the first week or two, don't try to hit the ball with all your force. Tennis coaches the world over give this advice, but people still tend to ignore it. I myself had a shoulder problem recently because I disregarded this rule. After a layoff I went right out and tried to play my usual game —and I paid dearly for it. The shoulder's all right now, but next time you can be sure that I'll work into top form more slowly.

If one of your main reasons for playing tennis is to exercise, then you may balk at having to exercise off the court. Especially early in the season, however, it's really a good idea to do at least a few exercises to prepare yourself.

It's not necessary to exhaust yourself. Just do a few exercises to limber up and to begin to tone your muscles. Before going to bed at night, or just after you get up in the morning, if you prefer, do a few sit-ups. The number you do depends on your age, weight, and general condition. Usually it's a good idea to at least do one or two more than you feel comfortable doing. Once you have strengthened your stomach, try adding a few leg lifts to your routine. Be careful not to overextend yourself. You might also do a few stretching exercises—the same general rules apply to determining how many you do.

One of the best all-around exercises for tennis is skipping rope. Skipping rope is good for toning muscles, building stamina, and developing coordination. Again, you'll have to use your own discretion as to how many to do, but you might start off with, say, 50 skips. Try to increase the number by 10 or 20 every day.

But remember, if you are out of shape, you can just as easily injure yourself doing exercises as you can playing tennis.

Women, especially smaller ones, can improve their game a great deal by using a squash ball. Squeezing a squash ball will strengthen the wrist and forearm—remember, you don't have to work at it so hard that you develop great, bulging muscles. Your aim is simply to tone the muscles. Every day, just squeeze the ball until your hand and arm get tired and then try to squeeze it, say, five times more. Almost every player in the world, man or woman, gets a sore hand and arm at the beginning of the season. Working with the squash ball for several weeks before you begin to play can help alleviate this problem.

At the beginning of the season or when you're just learning to play, another good exercise is to swing one or two rackets lightly. Go through all the strokes about 10 times daily for a week or so before you go out to play. This will help limber and tone shoulder, back, and arm muscles and will greatly lessen the chances of pulling or straining a muscle.

As I've said, doing a few exercises and starting off slowly will greatly lessen the chances of injury, but injuries will occur all the same. If you pull or strain a muscle or ligament, it's always best to check with a physician. The smallest, most inconsequential injury can often develop into something serious if not cared for properly. Once you know what kind of injury you have, you will know how to deal with it. Always follow doctor's orders.

Stiffness and minor aches and pains can usually be worked out with a bit of linament

Stretching exercises and leg lifts help
limber up and tone your muscles. It's not necessary
to exhaust yourself nor to exercise all day.

Skipping rope is one of the best all-around exercises for tennis. You can jump with both feet (above) or skip while jogging (right). Either method is effective.

and a massage. Swinging the racket lightly or jogging lightly can also help. A heat lamp can also benefit.

Strenuous muscle- and stamina-building exercises are best for the young, beginning player. Once you have developed your basic strength and stamina, they tend to stay with you. After that, agility and speed around the court need to be developed. I recommend sprinting and jumping exercises.

A very good exercise for quickness and agility is the exercise called shadow tennis. In shadow playing, you take your racket, go onto the court, and play an imaginary opponent. You should use all your usual footwork and usual strokes, but you should play at a much quicker pace than you would in an actual match. Starting at the center of the court, take two skips to the right and play a forehand. Then take two skips to the left and play a backhand, making sure to return to the center after each shot. Be sure always to make a definite shot and to bend your knees! After going right, then left, move in for a volley, then back for a smash, and then begin all over again. You can make this drill just as strenuous as you wish. Any time you begin to feel a bit lethargic and you want to get yourself going a bit, try spending about five minutes playing shadow tennis.

Another good exercise for agility is a jumping exercise I do. Simply jump into the air, arms extended in front of you but somewhat off to the side, and quickly bring your knees up to your chest. Again, you must judge for yourself how many repetitions you should do. Do them till you get tired and then try to do several more.

It's always important to warm up and to cool down slowly—especially early in the season or during training. I like to wear a track suit for training and practice. During chilly weather, wear one or two sweaters underneath your track suit. Take them off gradually as you warm up. For most people, it's not necessary to do limbering exercises before a match. The hitup before starting play is generally sufficient. After a match, get back into your warm things as quickly as possible. Try not to stand or sit around long after a match or a practice session. Keep moving until you can get into a warm shower. Especially during cool weather, I think it's a good idea to take vitamin C to avoid catching a cold or the flu.

When playing in hot weather, wear a light-colored hat. The hot sun on your head during a match can quickly sap your strength. And if the sun is hot enough, you'll really need the hat to prevent a case of sunstroke or heat exhaustion—both of which are pretty serious business. If these reasons aren't enough to convince you to wear a hat, then there's another good reason—the sun will dry out your hair and cause the ends to split.

Be careful to avoid sunburn. When you're involved in a match, you can easily forget about the sun; when the match is over, you may suddenly realize that you're badly

Shadow tennis will improve both your quickness
and agility. You play with neither ball nor
opponent, just your racket. Be sure to incorporate
all the movements you would make were
you playing a match—forehand, backhand, in for a
volley, back for a difficult overhead.

This jumping exercise is also good for improving agility. Extend your arms out front and to the side, and bring your knees up to your chest.

burned. Select a tanning preparation that will protect your particular complexion, and wear it when you play. If you use the kind that wipes off easily, then you should reapply it between games. Wearing makeup during a match can also help protect you from the sun. I've played in Australia when it's been 120 degrees on the court. With my face smeared with zinc cream, a wet handkerchief tied around my neck and a wet hat on my head, I presented quite a comical sight.

When the weather's hot, take a sip of water during the changeover. You need to replace some of the water you're losing, but I wouldn't advise drinking a whole glassful at a time. Also, in preparation for a match in hot weather, take a salt tablet or two. This helps reduce the chances of getting cramps.

There are no particular rules to follow in selecting equipment for yourself. It's simply a matter of personal preference—of finding what works for you, what you feel comfortable with. When choosing a racket, first find a grip that feels comfortable in your hand. After you've selected a grip, decide which kind of balance suits you. There are rackets with the weight in the grip, with the weight in the head, and with the weight evenly distributed. Any manufacturer can make its racket weighted a number of ways. Try each of them and pick the one that you feel the most comfortable with.

I personally prefer gut strings to nylon

strings. All of the other professional players do as well. Nylon is better under wet conditions, but it doesn't give as true a contact as the gut does. With gut strings, I feel that my racket performs more consistently and that I have more feel for the ball.

Most players prefer a tight racket, but the exact tension of the strings in your racket is again a matter of personal taste. If you're going to be playing on clay, it's a good idea to have your strings a bit looser than they would be for, say, a grass court. On clay you want the ball to stay on the strings for a longer time in order to gain control. On grass, you want more speed off the racket.

When selecting shoes, the same rule applies: Find the shoes that fit your feet. I prefer the particular shoe I wear because it gives a a lot of support to my ankle. There are a lot of quick stops and starts in tennis, and particularly when you're changing court surfaces every week, it is quite easy to injure an ankle. In fact, people have been known to break an ankle performing a simple maneuver on court. For this reason, I also wear elastic ankle supports for added protection. The elastic supports not only help keep me from turning an ankle, they also keep my legs from tiring as quickly as they normally would.

To get back to shoes, I think that weekend players prefer, and can get by with, a lighter shoe than that worn by most players who play daily. Each manufacturer, of course, makes its shoes a bit differently, so it's a

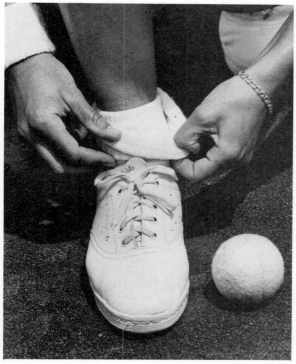

Some helpful equipment (clockwise from top left):
expensive sneakers with super support and
comfort, warm-up suits for cool days, a double pair
of socks to prevent blisters, a light-colored hat
to reflect heat and protect hair.

On hot days I like a reverse leather grip (far right), *which absorbs moisture. And I always wear a wristband* (below) *for the same reason.*

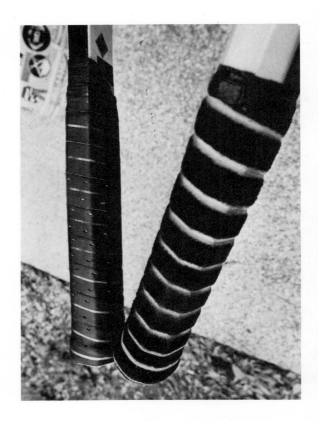

matter of shopping around until you find that brand that best suits your foot.

The frequency with which you replace your shoes will depend on how much you play. Stopping and starting and moving about on court will cause your shoes to stretch. Before long, your foot will begin to move about in them. I find that after three weeks or so, my toes have begun to hit up against the top of the shoe, so I change to new shoes about that often. The weekend player will, of course, find

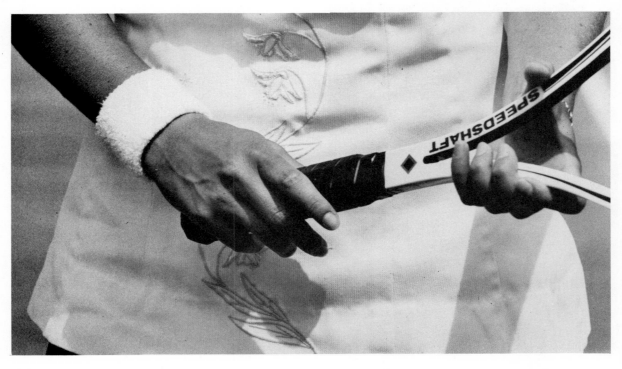

that her shoes last a good deal longer.

When I was first starting to play, my father advised me to wear two pairs of socks. I'm still following his advice, and I think it has helped me avoid problems with my feet. A lot of players have lost matches because they have developed blisters halfway through. It's amazing how many of the girls on the tour have trouble with their feet and have to go to a chiropodist to have calluses removed. When you make a sudden stop, as you do all the time in tennis, the two pairs of socks have a cushioning effect. They also help prevent blisters by eliminating movement in your shoe.

When the weather's hot, I think it's really necessary to wear a sweatband, at least on your racket hand. Without a sweatband, the moisture from your wrist and arm will get into the palm of your hand and make it very difficult for you to hold on to your racket.

Personally, I have difficulty with my grip when the weather is hot. Besides wearing a sweatband, I prefer to use a reverse leather grip. The reverse leather grip has a texture that is a bit like toweling. This particular grip wears out sooner than a regular grip, but it does make it easier to hold the racket when the weather is hot and your hand is moist.

I'm lucky enough to have been dressed by Teddy Tinling for the past several years. All his dresses are personally fitted, so I've had no problem in this area. I think, however, that when you're going out to buy a tennis dress in a shop, you should check the fit very closely, especially around the arms and around the shoulders. If the dress isn't fitted properly in these areas, you're quite likely to develop very sore spots where the dress rubs.

For practice, I like to wear shorts or a track suit, depending on the weather. In a match, however, you've got to be sure that your dress moves with you. A lot of the new synthetic materials, aside from being very hot to play in, will stick to you and hinder your movement. Choose a light material that allows freedom.

It may seem a minor point, but many women players select a different sort of undergarments to wear when they're playing. Be sure that your undergarments are flexible, that they don't hinder your movement, and that they don't chafe.

As I said in the very beginning, the amount of time and effort you devote to physical fitness will be determined by the type of tennis you wish to play. If you want to play competitive, tournament tennis, then you should spend a great deal of time off court developing your strength, stamina, and coordination. If you are interested in tennis mainly from the aspect of fun and exercise, then you needn't spend as much time on fitness.

In either case, however, you should use caution and common sense. Some injuries are unavoidable, but many can easily be prevented. Keeping fit will not only help you avoid injuries, it will increase your enjoyment of the game and enable you to play better.

TFW: Wrap-up

The Backhand
by Wendy Overton

Although most beginners shy away from the backhand and find it awkward, the backhand is actually the easiest stroke in tennis.

■ I feel you can get more power using the Eastern grip. The heel of your hand should be on the top of the racket handle. The index finger should be spread a bit more than the rest of the fingers, and the thumb should slide slightly up the side of the racket handle.

■ There are three parts to any tennis stroke —the backswing, making contact with the ball, and the follow-through. Even if only one of these ingredients is missing, the swing is not a proper stroke.

■ The left hand helps to take the racket back, and the right arm is fairly straight. Usually the backswing will come to a level about even with the left hip. The weight is on the right leg, and the right foot is at a 45-degree angle to the net.

■ Keeping the right arm comfortably straight and the racket perpendicular to the ground (your right arm and the racket handle should form a 110-degree angle) swing straight through. It is very important to keep a firm wrist throughout the stroke. You should make contact with the ball at about waist height. The entire backhand stroke describes an arc of 180 degrees.

■ The follow-through should continue through the ball and slightly upward so that the racket winds up pointing toward the net and slightly upward. Throughout, your weight should be on your right foot.

■ You should keep both your right shoulder and your head down. As you follow through, don't pull up.

■ There are three kinds of backhands—the flat drive, the topspin, the underspin. I hardly ever use a flat drive, opting for either spin shot to get the greatest degree of control and accuracy.

■ One of the most common mistakes made by beginners is jabbing at the ball. They tend to get their elbows in front of their bodies, which causes an erratic, jabbing motion. Beginners also have the problem of getting into the proper position.

■ Where you meet the ball determines the placement of your backhand. If you're going to go cross-court, you hit the ball a little bit earlier. If you're going to go down the line, you wait a bit. If you change your body position or realign your feet, you're going to give away your intentions to your opponent.

The Forehand
by Valerie Ziegenfuss

Every ball hit to you is a new experience; every ball is coming from a different angle at a different speed and is bouncing off a different part of the court surface. Every time you hit a tennis ball, you are faced with hundreds of variables. It only makes sense, then, that you should try to simplify your strokes rather than burden your mind with a lot of checkpoints.

■ The path in which the ball moves from the moment it strikes your opponent's racket to the moment it strikes yours is the "line of flight." It is this line of flight that the racket head must intercept in order to make the incoming ball go back into the court. Finding the correct line should always be done with the concept of the whole stroke in mind.

■ The pressure created by the ball against the racket head has a very identifiable feel. It is this "feel of the ball" that you need to learn and develop.

■ I use the Eastern, or "shake-hands" grip. I keep my hands close to my body because hitting is more comfortable and easier when it is done within the working area of my body. As I start the swing, I concentrate on the relation-

ship of my hand to the ball and on working the ball back into the target area. On contact there is a split second when I am not looking at the ball but at where I want the ball to go.

■ Many people say that you should meet the ball in front of your body. I disagree. The ball should only be *released* in front, where the follow-through imparts power to the stroke.

■ The racket head must generate the power and must be allowed to come through the ball completely if you are to gain the most control and power. This is an application of the formula for kinetic energy.

■ A general description of the way I hit a forehand: My body is in an open stance, my arm is bent, my elbow is close to my body, and my wrist is squared off to the ball. I hit the ball on the inside, which adds power and control. The racket comes over the ball at contact to impart topspin, and the follow-through is toward the inside of the ball.

■ I almost always hit a topspin forehand. As long as I'm hitting the ball with topspin, I don't want to flirt with the lines. When you start hitting balls that are in by inches, before long you are going to start hitting balls that are out by inches.

■ If you just remember the basic concept of putting the ball back into its line of flight and stop worrying about the "don'ts," you will be able to relax and enjoy the game. Tennis is very complicated, but it is, after all, a game and should be fun.

The Serve
by Lesley Hunt

The serve is a sort of throwing action, so the best way to begin to learn it is by throwing. Stand on the baseline and practice throwing the ball, either a real or imaginary one, into the service court.

■ Keep the fingers of the racket hand together—don't spread them too much or place the index finger up the handle. The heel of your hand should be against the heel of the racket.

■ Position your feet so that the line from the toe of the back foot to the toe of the front foot points in the direction in which you want the ball to go.

■ There are three basic kinds of serves— the flat serve, the spin serve, and the kicker, or American twist, serve. For each of these serves, the ball has to be thrown up to a slightly different spot—twelve o'clock for the kicker, one o'clock for the flat, two o'clock for the spinner.

■ As you begin the service action, your weight should be evenly distributed. Then, as you start to toss up the ball and begin to take your racket back, your weight should transfer to the back (right) foot. Be sure to look at the ball as you throw it up, and keep your eyes on it until the moment of impact. The racket arm should be at a comfortably full stretch as it goes down into the backswing. As the racket begins to come up into the Indian head position, your body should begin to move forward. All your weight should come through on the ball. The serve should be one smooth, continuous motion from start to finish.

■ You should keep a firm grip on the racket, but your wrist should be loose until the moment of impact. During the service action, your left shoulder should be pointing at the spot to which you're serving the ball.

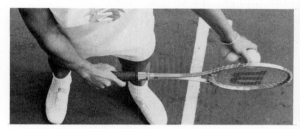

■ The ready position for receiving serve should be reasonably comfortable. Your feet should be slightly wider than the width of your shoulders, and your weight should be evenly distributed. The knees are flexed, and the body is in a sort of semicrouch position with the weight on the balls of the feet. The racket is held in front of the body with the neck of the racket held in the nonracket hand.

■ When returning serve to a net rusher, you must take a smaller backswing and a shorter stroke, and you should hit the ball farther in front of your body.

■ Don't try to overpower the ball when you're first learning or during the early part of the season. The muscles used in the serve— especially the back muscles—are muscles that don't normally undergo such strain.

The Overhead
by Karen Krantzcke

Most of the top professional girls smash with the backhand grip. With the backhand grip, it's easier to generate power and control.

■ It's important to get back into position quickly. When you hit the ball, it should be in front of your left foot (assuming you are right-handed). Therefore, when you hit the ball, you should be coming forward.

■ You're better balanced if both feet are on the ground when you hit the overhead.

■ Although the overhead is basically the same stroke as the serve, you have to dispense with the windup. The racket should be brought into place behind your head at the moment you begin to backpedal into position.

■ As you're backpedaling, your left, or nonracket, hand should be raised above your head, pointing at the ball. Raising your hand in this manner helps you to keep your balance and serves another important purpose—it helps you to keep your eyes on the ball. Your eyes should be on the ball from the moment you start to backpedal until the moment you hit the ball.

■ At the moment of contact, your head should be tilted back. You are watching the ball. Your head should remain in this position until the ball has left the strings. Many players will drop their heads just before or just as they hit the ball. This causes mistakes.

■ Your racket arm should be fully extended when you make contact with the ball. On the overhead power comes from the shoulder; the minute you bend your elbow, you lose power and your overhead will tend to float. After you make contact with the ball, swing right through.

■ Generally, you should be trying for the flat smash. If you can't put the ball away, then try to vary your attack by using the slice

smash. Reserve the topspin smash for those times when the ball is behind you and there's nothing else you can do with it.

■ You should almost always aim your smash to your opponent's backhand.

■ On lobs that are especially good or high, it's best to let the ball bounce first. Generally, your ensuing overhead will not be an outright winner, but it can be hit with slice and strategically placed.

■ One of the common mistakes that tennis players make is trying for extra power on the overhead. If you grit your teeth and try to kill the ball, you'll only start missing shots.

The Volley
by Rosemary Casals

The main thing to think about at first is to meet the ball in front of your body. To develop a feel for the volley, a beginner will usually start by simply catching the ball. After she's become proficient at stopping or catching the ball with her bare hand, then she can begin to practice with a racket. This transition can be made quite smoothly if the beginner keeps in mind that the racket is merely an extension of the hand.

■ The volley should always be hit toward the baseline. A good volley should be hit in front of the body and pushed out to an area close to a foot from the baseline.

■ It's important to get to the ball in time to position yourself to make the shot. If you're going to your right to make a forehand volley (assuming that you're right-handed) your left foot should be in front. Conversely, on the backhand volley, your right foot should be in front.

■ Don't change the position of the racket during the volley. The racket head should remain more or less perpendicular to the ground. The racket head should never be twisted before it meets the ball.

■ Never swing on a volley. The volley should be a blocking action.

■ Many players have a tendency to place the thumb of their racket hand on the back of the grip when hitting the backhand or backhand volley. I wouldn't advise this.

■ When hitting the volley, you should try to utilize the speed your opponent has given the ball. It's not necessary to hit an extremely crisp volley. The more important thing is placement.

■ When you hit a volley, generally your arm should be extended well in front of you and your wrist should be locked. But as in all tennis shots, you have to be flexible.

■ On the low volley, bend your knees. You've got to get right down to the ball so that your eyes are almost on a level with the racket and the ball.

■ Generally, a put-away volley will be cross-court. For instance, when you're coming to net after serving and the ball comes to you on the forehand side, your put-away shot will be cross-court. On the backhand side, the same general rule applies.

■ The volley is an offensive shot. When you're at the net, you should be attacking at all times—and I feel that a player should get to the net every chance she has. When you're at net, you've cut off your opponent's angles and given her less room to hit the ball past you. Be aggressive with all volleys.

The Lob and the Dropshot
by Kerry Reid

In men's tennis the lob you see most often is the offensive, topspin lob. Women, however, don't move back as well as men. Because of this, the undercut, defensive lob (which is much easier to hit) usually gets the job done quite well.

■ If possible, you should try to position yourself with your side to the net and play the lob the same way you would a normal forehand or backhand.

■ Remember to keep the racket head low. Drop the racket head below the level of your wrist, get the racket head right under the ball, and open the face of the racket. Having the racket face open as you strike the ball imparts underspin.

■ Keep your backswing to a minimum—all you need is a small, circular motion to get your racket moving. Keep your eyes on the ball. Don't be timid in hitting the lob. It is better to lose the point by hitting the lob long than it is to hit the lob short and let your opponent blast you off the court with her overhead.

■ Normally, the best place to hit the lob is on the diagonal—to either the forehand corner or the backhand corner. Of the two corners, I much prefer the backhand corner.

■ If you've hit a good lob, you should always follow it to the net, unless you are too far out of position to do so.

■ If the wind is blowing from your left to your right and you want to hit to the backhand corner, you may have to aim for the center of the court. If the wind is from your right to your left, you may have to hit the ball actually outside the court and let the wind bring the ball in. When the wind is blowing lengthwise down the court and is at your back, don't try to lob.

■ If you're playing a short opponent, you should lob more.

■ The grip for the forehand dropshot is the Eastern grip, and for the backhand dropshot, it is the Continental grip.

■ The dropshot should never be attempted from near the baseline, and the backswing should be short and deliberate. Your body, if possible, should be side-on to the net. Keep your eye on the ball. The racket face should be open—tilted upward—as you make contact with the ball. The racket comes under the ball as you swing. The swing itself is at about half the speed of the normal groundstroke.

■ The follow-through should be along the flight of the ball, and you should hit through the ball. Decide what you're going to do with the ball, and then do it. Dropshots that are slapped, poked or hit half-heartedly wind up in the net more often than not.

Court Strategy
by Nancy Richey

Court strategy can be divided into two categories—serving strategy and receiving strategy. In either situation one basic rule applies: Keep your weight forward. Many players have a tendency to lean backward, a mistake that costs them mobility.

■ When I'm planning to serve and volley, I try to hit my serve into the T formed by the center and back service lines. In other words, if my opponent is right-handed, I hit to her backhand side when I'm serving to the deuce court and to her forehand side when I'm serving to the ad court.

■ When I serve down the middle to the deuce court and go to net, my opponent has three possible shots: cross-court to my forehand, down the line to my backhand, or a lob. If she cross-courts or hits down the line, my volley will be cross-court.

■ If you want to vary your serve occasionally, aim for the center of the back service line, directly at your opponent.

■ One of the fundamentals of court strategy is to keep your opponent always moving. Once you have your opponent moving, you want to make her reverse direction as often as possible. In other words get her moving one way, and then hit the ball the other.

■ Be aggressive and take the net when your opponent makes a miscue during a rally. If, during a rally your opponent hits short, you should attack. Hit the ball down the line or to the deep middle—but still on her backhand

side—and go to the net. Your best approach shot is almost always down the line.

■ If your opponent is attempting to serve and volley, the foremost idea in your head should be to keep the ball as low as possible as it clears the net, no matter what side of the court you elect to return to. It's much more difficult for her to hit a good volley from a low position than from a high one.

■ If the server serves and then stays back, the receiver should play the ball high—say five or six feet over the net—in order to utilize the depth of the court.

■ Knowing your opponent can be an invaluable aid in making tactical decisions on the court. Almost every player has certain patterns of play; everyone has a favorite shot from a given position. Be especially alert during the early stages of a match. Watch for patterns and quirks, and catalog them.

■ Also watch for your opponent's strengths, and keep away from them.

■ Whenever you're down game point, no matter what the situation, never hit a dropshot and never try for a screaming winner. Play it safe. The time to be aggressive is when you're ahead.

Doubles
by Betty Stöve

Forming a true partnership with your partner is very important in doubles. It's crucial that there be sympathy and good understanding. If there is any sort of friction between the partners, then a mistake made by either is likely to cause ill feelings, which in turn cause you to lose matches, confidence, enjoyment—and your partner.

■ Doubles has become essentially a net game. If you want to play good tennis you must come to the net, get into position, and put the ball away with a volley.

■ Look for a partner who balances your game. If you are erratic, find a steady partner.

■ When you come to net, get as close to it as possible. Try to avoid leaving open corners that will allow your opponents to exploit the wider angles of the doubles court. At the same time, always be aware of the threat down the middle of the court. Be alert, and be ready to move in either direction.

■ When playing against net rushers who come to net on every point, your best strategy is to hit a lot of high lobs and loopy drives.

■ When you don't know what to do with the ball, use the safe shots. Hit the ball down the middle, hit a lob, stay away from dropshots, try to use the width of the court at all times, and avoid making silly mistakes.

■ The partner with the stronger serve should serve first, unless there is one left-handed player and one right-handed player and there is bright sun. Then the side of the court will determine who serves first.

■ If you are able to play the various kinds of serves—the flat, the slice, the twist—you should mix up your serves. This same principle applies to return of service. Keep your opponents in a situation that demands that they expect almost anything at any time.

■ When you're receiving serve, try to stand in the line that you expect the serve to follow. If the server moves to her right, then you should move to your right; if she moves to her left, move to your left.

■ On crossovers never move before your opponent has hit the ball. As you move laterally along the net, your partner should also move laterally to cover the part of the court you have just vacated. Be sure to go all the way on the crossover.

■ The better player of a partnership should play in the backhand court as much as possible so that she can take shots down the middle as well as a majority of the lobs.

■ Remember that tennis is just a game and that you're out there to have fun. Never get angry or upset with your partner. Encourage her, congratulate her on her good shots, commiserate with her on her bad ones.

Mixed Doubles
by Françoise Dürr

In mixed doubles the man is normally the stronger player. As such, he should take all the more difficult shots. He should hit the majority of the overheads and do the majority of the poaching, or crossing over. Conversely, the weakest part of the team is usually the woman. Therefore, when playing mixed doubles, you should try to play the ball to the woman opponent as much as possible.

■ Power is not as important in doubles as it is in singles. Hit the ball into a deep corner, or hit it on a sharp angle. Hitting the ball with all your might in doubles is a waste of energy and causes you to make mistakes.

■ Every time you hit a shot, you should be aware of where your partner is on the court, what your partner is doing, and how your shot will affect your partner.

■ The crossover is a difficult move for beginners, but because it is such a basic tactic in doubles, I recommend that beginners attempt it from the very start.

■ If your opponents are poaching a great deal and are successful at it, try to hit a few hard returns down the alley. This is a difficult shot and not really a high percentage shot, but even if you miss, you've served a purpose.

■ When you are at net and your partner is receiving serve, your eyes should be on the opponent who is at net.

■ When playing at net while your partner is serving, your position should be two or three feet from the sideline and a yard or two from the net. The distance between you and the net is crucial.

■ In doubles it's very important that you get your first serve in. It's not as important that the serve be a powerful one. Hit the first service deep, and be sure that it goes in.

■ When going to net from backcourt, you should always try to get past the service line. The area between the baseline and the service line should be avoided as much as possible. When you are in this area, almost anything your opponents hit to you will be difficult to return.

■ If the man in the ad court overpowers you with a return of serve to your backhand every time you serve to him, talk to your partner and suggest the Australian tandem. In the Australian tandem, your partner, rather than standing in the opposite court from you, stands in the same court.

■ Sometimes you may make an exceptional shot and set up a winner that your partner then puts away. You may feel he gets too much credit for this, but this is the way the game should be played. Expect it and accept it. On-court harmony is the key to a successful doubles partnership.

Physical Fitness and Equipment
by Kerry Harris

Being physically fit greatly reduces your chances of injury. Moreover, if you should happen to sustain an injury, being physically fit will help you to recover both quickly and completely.

■ For the beginner, or for the weekend player who is starting after a layoff, the important thing is to begin slowly. For the first week or two, don't try to hit the ball with all your force. Tennis coaches the world over give this advice, but people still tend to ignore it.

■ It is a good idea to do a few off-court exercises to prepare yourself for on-court play. It's not necessary to exhaust yourself. Just do a few exercises to limber up and to begin to tone your muscles. When doing exercise, no matter which one you choose, it's helpful to do at least one or two more than you feel comfortable doing.

■ Recommended exercises include sit-ups, leg lifts, skipping rope, squeezing a squash ball to strengthen the wrist, and jumping exercises. Shadow tennis is also a very good exercise for quickness and agility.

■ It's always important to warm up and to cool off slowly, especially early in the season or during training. I like to wear a track suit for training and practice. For most people it's not necessary to do limbering up exercises before a match. The hitup before starting play is generally sufficient.

■ When playing in hot weather, wear a light-colored hat. Be careful to avoid sunburn.

When it's really hot, a wet handkerchief tied around your neck helps a lot. And don't be afraid to take a little water each time you change courts.

■ Choosing a racket depends on what feels comfortable to you, both in grip and in balance. Although nylon stringing is better suited to wet weather, every professional has her racket strung with gut.

■ I prefer a sneaker that gives extra support to my ankles. However, a weekend player may not need that much support. Wearing two pairs of socks will prevent blisters.

■ When the weather's hot, it's necessary to wear a sweatband. You might even want to try using a reverse leather grip, which absorbs moisture very well.

■ Many women players select a different sort of undergarment to wear when they're playing. Be sure that your undergarments are flexible, that they don't hinder your movement, and that they don't chafe.

■ Use caution and common sense. Some injuries are unavoidable, but many can be easily prevented. Keeping fit will not only help you to avoid injuries, it will increase your enjoyment of the game and enable you to play better.